Dreadful Quietude

A confused saturation
of Pre 9/11 America & Supermen

By Geoffrey Gatza

BlazeVOX [books]

Buffalo, New York

Dreadful Quietude, A confused saturation of Pre 9/11 America & Supermen
by Geoffrey Gatza

Copyright © 2004

Published by BlazeVOX [books]

Printed in the United States of America

Book design by Geoffrey Gatza
Cover art by Abraham Harboring

First Edition

ISBN   0-9759227-1-8 ISBN 13   978-0-9759227-1-2
Library of Congress Control Number: 2004116045

BlazeVOX [books]
14 Tremaine Ave
Kenmore, NY 14217

Editor@blazevox.org

publisher of weird little books

BlazeVOX [books]

blazevox.org

2   4   6   8   0   9   7   5   3   1

Acknowledgements for *Dreadful Quietude*:

The Author would like to thank the editors of the following journals for publishing and promoting this work Exquisite Corpse; VeRT, Blackbox; Sidereality; Znine, xStream; BlazeVOX; Peanut Butter Review; Jack in the Box.

I wish to thank Kent Johnson for his encouragement, Ted Pelton and Ethan Paquin, Michael Kelleher, especially Robert Creeley for not laughing at this project and all of the other Buffalo Poets. God Bless America, Whitman's America, Mythic America, may we see you again ....

I wish to dedicate this book with affection to Kathy Boone, for being kind to cats. And with admiration to N., my far away place of neverwhere ponds.

Dreadful Quietude

A confused saturation
of Pre 9/11 America & Supermen

Every true poet is a monster.

--Tomaz Salamun

I may have my faults, but
being wrong ain't one of them.

--Jimmy Hoffa

In 1955, Charles Olson wrote two letters to the young poet Ed Dorn, later revised as A Bibliography on America for Ed Dorn. I read this compilation in the late 1960s. At one point, Olson argued:

> PRIMARY DOCUMENTS. And to hook on here is a lifetime of assiduity. Best thing to do is to dig one thing or place or man until you yourself know more abt that than is possible to any other man. It doesn't matter whether it's Barbed Wire or Pemmican or Paterson or Iowa. But exhaust it. Saturate it. Beat it. And then U KNOW everything else very fast: one saturation job (it might take 14 years). And you're in, forever.

His admonition is to Dorn as a novice, and rings with a certainty that I can only partially share. But it planted a seed in me for the writing of this book. My aim is not to know more than "is possible to any other man," but to make use of a pluralistic approach that may result in a fuller "reading" of comic book imaginations might yield. I don't want to engage the comics in an ahistorical void or to strip mine them for "poetic" materials. Among other things, I want to incorporate their imagery into poetry as a primary antecedent dimension, in effect opening a trap door in poetry's floor onto these unbounded but evocative gestures. As a poet's book, *Superman* is an attempt to reclaim the poem merged with drawing of Blake and the phanopoeia of Pound as imagistic-mythical memory in which early intimations of what we call "muse" may be experienced. Poetry itself is questioned throughout this book: how can one make use of its strategies to engage materials that have no historical significance or penetrating language?

Enjoy!

Geoffrey Gatza

Prelude

London, 1879

home of Thomas Carlyle

And how should such a poem begin
In light, a Blaze, exploding sparks set adrift over dried fiber

A dark room
two men sit in wing'd chairs
from the next room ... A rustle
"Clarice, is that you. Come in and stoke our fire, now there's a good girl"

"Is this one"

"Yes, I hired her on only to torment her for the rest of my life."

"Well that goes beyond the good and *the* evil, now doesn't it. The French Revolution will
never be the same, will it." He snickers

"It was ... Is, I should say" stammers
he turns to the door. "Clarice, you're not looking for paper scraps again are you?"

A long creak, stems of light grow
The door opens and an old form enters.

"In the beginning was the Word, and
the Word was with God, and the
Word was God." says she as she pokes life into the fire "No paper words shall burn by me
again, will they now sir" she pokes

"Yes, yes" grumbles the man, "The same as was in the beginning .... with God."

"All things were made by him; and
without him was not any thing made
that was made." Calls from the other chair "In him was life; and the life was the light of men."

"And the light shineth in darkness;
and the darkness comprehended it
not." finishes she

"And it's John whom we can all come home to. The most poetic of all who claim to be of
god's hand, most heroic too."

A long pshaw fluttering from the wing'd chair to the left. "Thomas, the christian faith serves only to hamper human potential and has no basis on our everyday experiences"

"Fredrick" he says after a long pause, "If Jesus Christ were to come today, people would not crucify him. They would ask him to dinner, and hear what he had to say, and make fun of it. However, the Poet is a heroic figure belonging to all ages; whom all ages possess."

"It is true, there could be a metaphysical world; the absolute possibility of it is hardly to be disputed. We behold all things through the human head and cannot cut off this head; while the question nonetheless remains what of the world would still be there if one had cut it off."

"No sadder proof can be given by a man of his own littleness than disbelief in great men."

"Convictions are dangerous enemies of truth, more so than lies."

"The great law of culture is:
let each become all that he was created capable of being."

And the fires grew in his eyes, and began,

"I shall tell you my thoughts on the three metamorphoses of the spirit: I see the metaphor of the spirit as a being that changes over time. As a camel; and the camel to change to a lion; and the lion change to child.

the spirit always faces difficulties,
the strong, reverent spirit can bear a great deal:
but the difficult and the most difficult are
what its strength demands.
What is difficult? asks the spirit that can bear a great deal,
and kneels down like a camel wanting to be well loaded.

What is most difficult, O heroes, asks the spirit that can bear these things that I may take it upon myself and give praise to my strength?
Is it not humbling oneself to wound one's arrogance?
Letting one's folly shine to mock one's wisdom?...

Or is it this: stepping into filthy waters when they are the waters of truth, and not be disgusted by the cold frogs and hot toads?

Or is it this: loving those that despise us and offering a hand to the ghost that would frighten us?

All these most difficult things the spirit that can bear great things
takes upon itself: like the camel, while weighed down, speeds into the desert, as does the spirit speed into its dark desert.

In the darkest of desert, however, the second metamorphosis occurs:
here the spirit becomes a lion who would conquer his freedom
and be master in his own desert.

Here he seeks out his last master:
he wants to fight him and his last god;
for ultimate victory he wants to fight with the great dragon.

Who is the great dragon whom the spirit will no longer call lord and god?

"Thou shalt" is the name of the great dragon.

16

But the spirit of the lion says, "I will."
"Thou shalt" lies in his way,
sparkling like gold,
an animal covered with scales;
and on every scale shines a golden
     "thou shalt."
     Values, thousands of years old, shine on these scales; and thus speaks the
mightiest of all dragons:

     "All value has long been created, and I am all created value. Verily, there shall be
no more 'I will.'" Thus speaks the dragon.

     My brothers, why is there a need in the spirit for the lion?

Why is not the beast of burden, which renounces and is reverent, enough?

To create new values -- that even the lion cannot do; but the creation of freedom for oneself
and a sacred **"No"** even to duty -- for that, my brothers, the lion is needed.

To assume the right to new values –
that is the most terrifying assumption
for a reverent spirit bearing great things.

Verily, to him it is preying,
and a matter for a beast of prey.
He once loved "thou shalt" as most sacred:
     now he must find illusion and caprice even in the most sacred, that freedom from
his love may become his prey: the lion is needed for such prey.

But say, what can the child do that even the lion could not do?

Why must the preying lion still become a child?
The child is innocence and forgetting,
a new beginning, a game,

a self-propelled wheel,
a wheel moving from its center

a first movement,
a sacred **"Yes."**

For the game of creation, Thomas, a sacred "Yes" is needed:
the spirit now wills his own will,
and he who had been lost to the world now conquers the world."

"Religion is indeed an Allegory, a Symbol of what men felt and knew about the Universe; and
all Religions are symbols of that, altering always as that alters:

but it seems to me a radical perversion,
and even inversion, of the business,
to put that forward as the origin and moving cause,
when it was rather the result and termination.

To get beautiful allegories, a perfect poetic symbol,
was not the want of men; but to know what they were to believe
about this Universe, what course they were to steer in it;

what, in this mysterious Life of theirs,
they had to hope and to fear,
to do and to forbear doing.

The Pilgrim's Progress is an Allegory, and a beautiful, just and serious one: but consider
whether Bunyan's Allegory could have *preceded* the Faith it symbolizes!

The Faith had to be already there, standing believed by everybody;
of which the Allegory could *then* become a shadow; and, with all its seriousness, we may
say a *sportful* shadow, a mere play of the Fancy,
in comparison with that awful Fact and scientific certainty which it poetically strives to
emblem.

The Allegory is the product of the certainty, not the producer of it; not in Bunyan's nor in any
other case.

You remember that fancy of Plato's,
of a man who had grown to maturity in some dark distance,

and was brought on a sudden into the upper air to see the sun rise.
What would his wonder be, his rapt astonishment at the sight
we daily witness with indifference!

With the free open sense of a child,
yet with the ripe faculty of a man,

his whole heart would be kindled by that sight,
he would discern it well to be Godlike, his soul would fall
down in worship before it.

What in such a time as ours
it requires a Prophet or Poet to teach us,
namely, the stripping-off of those poor
undevout wrappages, nomenclatures and scientific hearsays,

this, the ancient earnest soul,
as yet unencumbered with these things,
did for itself.

Worship is transcendent wonder;
wonder for which there is now no limit or measure;

that is worship.
To primeval men,

all things and everything they saw
exist beside them were an emblem of the Godlike,
of some God.

Well; these truths were once more readily felt than now. The young
generations of the world, who had in them the freshness of young children,
and yet the depth of earnest men, who did not think that they had finished
off all things in Heaven and Earth by merely giving them scientific names,

but had to gaze direct
at them there,

18

with awe and wonder:

they felt better what of divinity is in man and Nature;
they, without being mad, could _worship_ Nature,
and man more than anything else in Nature.

Worship, that is, as I said above, admire without limit: this, in the full
use of their faculties, with all sincerity of heart, they could do.

It is well said, in every sense, that a man's religion is the chief fact
with regard to him. A man's, or a nation of men's. By religion I do not
mean here the church-creed which he professes, the articles of faith which
he will sign and, in words or otherwise, assert; not this wholly, in many
cases not this at all. We see men of all kinds of professed creeds attain
to almost all degrees of worth or worthlessness under each or any of them.

This is not what I call religion, this profession and assertion; which is
often only a profession and assertion from the outworks of the man, from
the mere argumentative region of him, if even so deep as that.

But the thing a man does practically believe (and this is often enough *without* asserting it
even to himself, much less to others); the thing a man does practically lay to heart, and know
for certain, concerning his vital
relations to this mysterious Universe, and his duty and destiny there, that
is in all cases the primary thing for him, and creatively determines all
the rest.

That is his religion;
or, it may be,

his mere skepticism and no-religion: the manner it is in which he feels himself to be
spiritually related to the Unseen World or No-World; and I say, if you tell me what that is, you
tell me to a very great extent what the man is, what the kind of things he will do is.

This is manifest to the meanings of Heroism;
the divine relation (for I may well call it such)
which in all times unites a Great Man to other men;

One comfort is, that Great Men,
taken up in any way,
are profitable
company.

We cannot look, however imperfectly, upon a great man,
without gaining something by him.

He is the living light-fountain, which it is
good and pleasant to be near.
The light which enlightens, which has enlightened the darkness

of the world; and this not as a kindled lamp only,
but rather as a natural luminary shining by the gift of Heaven;

a flowing light-fountain, as I say,
of native original insight,
of manhood and heroic nobleness

in whose radiance all souls feel that it is well with them.
On any terms whatsoever,

I consider Hero-worship
to be the grand modifying element in that ancient system of thought.

What I called the perplexed jungle of Paganism sprang,
we may say, out of many roots: every admiration, adoration of a star
or natural object, was a root or fiber of a root;

but Hero-worship is the deepest root of all;
the tap-root, from which in a great degree all
the rest were nourished and grown.

And now if worship even of a star had some meaning in it,
how much more might that of a Hero!

Worship of a Hero is transcendent admiration of a Great Man.
I say great men are still admirable;
I say there is, at bottom, nothing else admirable!

No nobler feeling than this of admiration
for one higher than himself dwells in the breast of man.

It is to this hour, and at all hours, the vivifying influence in man's life.

Religion I find stand upon it.
Hero-worship,

| heartfelt | prostrate | admiration, |
| submission, | burning, | boundless, |

for a noblest godlike Form of Man,

is not that the germ of Christianity itself?

The greatest of all Heroes is One--whom we do not name here!
Let sacred silence meditate that sacred matter;

you will find it the ultimate perfection of a principle
extant throughout man's whole history on earth.

Canto 36

FDR reelected
The WPA
Eugene O'Neil accepts Nobel Prize

Jesse Owens
non.fictional american hero

the world's fastest runner
was born on an Alabama farm

son of a sharecropper
grandson of a slave

a dreamer
dreamed the dreams of others
gave hope to millions
individual excellence

Oval of the Olympic legends
verse race or national origin
cold and rainy

elected captain Ohio State University track team
first black to hold such position on any Ohio State Team

Jesse Owens became the fourth American to capture three or more championships in one Olympic-meet.

stunning victories of four gold medals
at the 1936 Olympic games in Berlin

August 3
Won the broad jump medal
leaping 25' 10 1/4" inches

August 5
he broke the world and Olympic record
in the 200-meter dash

August 9
Lead-off man 400-meter relay team
which won in record breaking time

discredited claims made by Adolph Hitler
no Negro would beat a German

to receiving the official Nazi Swastika
from Adolph Hitler

After receiving this honor
Owens went to the radio
extending greetings to his folks
                    back home in America

           returned home aboard the Queen Mary
           amidst wild cheers and applause from
           all people
                    of all races
                            all colors
                                    and all nationalities

           Owens turned down cash offers to turn professional
           but wished to finish his college education

           The Chicago Defender reads:
           Jesse Owens is the god of the sports fans here…

Canto 37

Amelia Earhart disappears

Do what you will! This is the talk of the Hermit, the Lover, and the man of Earth. They all come together, sit back and talk of constraint and eventually come to a conclusion, then stray; as stars in the nights. This is the talk. The word of sin is constraint. This is what they say. They come together talk, solve then do nothing with the answers they are given. They will do no wrong, if you look closely into the word. But how can they do right? The sin is constraint and that constraint is self imposed. I don't always agree with them. They do not always agree with each other. That's the moral; if one needs a moral, here it is set down in a beginning, a beginning hunted like the snark.

This shall be a moral of the whole. It is of course a moral utterance. It is derivative in form and conception from Rabelais, for it was him who placed this moral over the fictional Abbey of Thélème. The classic satire in *Gargantua,* by François Rabelais, a French priest and occultist. Study Rabelais before discussing morality. In Rabelais this rule "fay çe que vouldras", translates "to do what you will." This is a part of my literary life and culture. It is my life. It is my role. It is the way of the True and Right Order Medmenham Friars. So it shall be.

It is an authority, set in place by an author, told through a character, to an author then reintegrated back into the system by a narrator setting the stage for a character speaking for a real person who is not that person at all. Do what you will, is explained in terms of true will, the ultimate being, the spiritual core of each person, as a divine self-ordained path through the world of experience, intangible and other.

Do what you will refers not to the outer emotional and intellectual self but to an aurora of personal divinity. And divinity is often never divine. Often, will is contrasted with whim, and the knowing and doing of the true objective will is a prisoner printing license plates, painted not in terms of license but of responsibility and consequence, as its result. These are apparent.

These are also apparent contradictions. And so the moral takes on a different meaning, a non-dual meaning. It has to, that is if it is to work, it must. How else can one enter into something without some form of reconciliation. The realization of one's true nature comes at the same time that one realizes one's unity with all beings. How does one cross the gap, gap the bridge, bridge a relatively unenlightened form to a state of pure asymetrix; which is also paradoxically selfless.

At different levels there are different criteria of truth. The truth is one of three; three blind mice. The truth is never a clear chop from the butcher's wife, now is it? The truth of one is sacred to that one, and is false or nonsense to another. Do what you will is the moral; and the law is amoral; it is all constraint. It's the only constraint, all else becomes sheets riding against the wind. So for the ordinary person, do what you will is a useful rule of thumb. At higher levels one realizes that there are no ordinary persons, or that the distinction between self and other is an illusion. There is no self yet there is self. There are no others, yet my neighbors are closing in. These are contradictions. Here it is set down in the beginning, a beginning hunted like in the dark.

*   *   *

One supposes you can see the world as light breaking over waterfalls as a shade close to that of mousepad blue. I know this like I know nothing else. I know you, understand why you need to do what it is that you do. I haven't known this in anyone. I know you. I know nothing else and yet there you are knowing me as I know you. You are red.

Every story needs a contextual understanding in order to arrive at the correct interpretation. If not things breakdown from the illogical nature of the beast. This is why the church employs priests; also the reason protestants protested … that and the mistresses and general bawdiness altogether. Not the point, but a start … The story need to follow a logic so all can understand and be understood. This is universal. However, understand that all meaning is not universal. Being is born from and in the self, and that self is conscious. The consciousness is a biological function as wondrous as defecation, and as dull as digestion. And this process is as unique to me as your process is unique to you. I will never understand you completely and you, I.

So how do you prevent an infinite breakdown when interpreting me? Or a rule, or for that matter a representation of anything? No rule or meaning is self-interpreting, that much is clear. No idea is truly as clear to the author as it is to the reader. The two never meet. It is here an understanding of Keats becomes important. If you have never thought of him outside of a ninth grade lit course – you will not understand me, my life, or what I accomplish. This is ok. Grecian urns break when not kept away from cats.

The line that divides knowing how things are and knowing how to do things is evident to all parties involved. This is the way things are. The things we never forget, and base all other things against.

One first learns the basics of balance by being taught certain rules, and, after having stood upright enough times, no longer is mindful of those rules but instead lets the body take over. And from this standing erect we see the world not as a beast, not dangling from a tree, but as authority. Authority towering over the others.

Its at this point it becomes dirty. The story can no longer apologize for itself. It can only become. And for it to become, true or otherwise we need a backdrop, an oil cloth of sorts to spare the floor further mudding. It's the great city among great cities: Metropolis. Representing America at large. An old port city down on its luck. It means everything yet says nothing. Metropolis is violence in every subdivision of red bound to our spectrum of culture. A forgetting arrow moving in quivers. We experience, enjoy, feel whatever it is we feel, then shoot on to bigger targets.

Golden
Age
of
Comics

Canto 38

The Holocaust
August first appearance of Superman in Action comics

I remember a time when I knew what happiness was …

And so it is as it should
be
beginning in action

Beyond words
twisting in turn, its primal being

an evensong of night

image
drawn in
words

a tale told in pale yellow

episodic mother whispers

enter the womb of creation
a narrative cave

our comic book pulp
chopped newsprint sweating acid

He holds a green sedan over head
a muscular white man dressed in authoritative blue
captured in the moment
saving

a red cape fluttering
a man's arms raised
woman   aghast
in a pill box hat covers her   screams

There is nothing unreasonable or unnatural
about our Superman fantasies.

They are spinning out of control
and that's all there is too it. If she just gives me
what I ask for then nothing will happen.

lumbering man holding
in shadows

a white hair woman
her mouth
gloved

She shoved me. Fuck her. I shoved her back. Give me the purse.	No she still holds on to her shiny black bag as if that's all she has left in this here world. Look around this place! You have so much and I have so damn little, so give me the cash money that's in the bag. I don't want your credit cards, I don't want your personal numbers; I want your cash and then I will leave!

It was that simple. Terror again.
She remembered the times she had witnessed people beaten in their homes.
That was over race.

For that reason,
and that reason alone
she and her now late husband packed a bag and left Montgomery.

	this action was for money and money alone.
But this attack, happening now was hatred of another kind;	

She didn't have any money of her own. Not in cash, anyway. Nothing to pacify him.
He was looking for an avenue to get high and would beat her again to get there.

Bent over like an animal pausing in an attack, arms angling out on his knees, ready to lunge. He was breathing hard now. She couldn't see it but he needed to breath. He couldn't catch his breath after her kick. She, now on the floor, huddled over top of her handbag, unwilling as ever to give up anything of herself.
"Fuck him!" she seethed

One of Superman's most deeply held convictions 　　　　he must never use his superpowers for profit or personal gain. 　　　　has always rejected compensation for his super-heroic performance, 　　　　he has, on occasion, for the promise of contributions to charity, grandstanded.	Superman is a man of high ideals, his behavior is motivated by an enduring sense of honor and principle. 　　　　Superman's most deeply held conviction is the blessedness of human life. 　　　　This character trait forbids him from ever taking a human life, 　　　　even that of the worst of villains.

Skip was angry now. He wondered how many times he would have to hit her. He knew a tough woman when he met one, and she was tough; but not that tough. He rose from his knees taking a deep breath though his wide nostrils and moved towards the old woman. How long before loosing her cash held less value than loosing her teeth. She shrieked back into the nearby white walled corner and formed a ball, making the purse her center. It was going to be a battle of wills from this point forward.

It is normal to use imagination
to aspire to power and dominate
the surrounding environment.

There is no surprise that many men
fantasize about having the power
to do as they dream

Superman is that fantasy's
        culmination
        and practice.

Superman
is that fantasy's culmination and practice.

His superior senses give him a
commanding confidence
and respect from man and beast, alike.

He sees the ultimate good as performing acts of justice in a colorform red world of clearly drawn blue images of good versus evil.

Superman always keeps his word

Superman always keeps his word
it's against his philosophy to resist the law,
even when the law seems unreasonable or unjust.

Superman is vigorously opposed to
one-armed bandits, blackjack,
and all other forms of gambling.

the practice is a parasitic vice that has no place in a decent town.

There is no greater
american, living or drawn.

His hands fumbled through
a slicked black coated red
wad of bills.

It was mostly singles but
there was a twenty in there;
he saw that for sure.

And maybe it was a
hundred. How fucking great
would that be?
A hundred
with the twenty and the
singles would set him up
for at least three weeks.

He would get out of town in style.

Skip didn't recognize what room they were in.
He had to get out of here. She would wake up soon.
She wasn't moving. And mixed with the blood coming from her nose was green fluid he had never seen before.
She might be dead. "Oh fuck" he thought.
He killed the old woman. If she only did what he said. She must have been eighty. He shouldn't have knocked around so hard. But he was enraged. It was her fault. That he was sure of. But he had to get out … now!

Blind with fright he ran down the stairs with an open fist pushing everything out of his way. His hand caught the high boy and a collection of dishes and figurines crashed to the floor. He stepped on a wedgewood blue flower urn. His foot swerved on the white figures emblazoned on the broken pieces and he fell. They were greek figures chasing something … that something was now unrecognizably shattered. He thought of love.

He had to get out now! He was frighten. His heart quickened. Beating, pulsing, crashing to the sounds of his violence.
He got up and ran.

A door appeared off to his left. He pushed for it; as he exited he knocked over a lamp with his knee.

On the street all was calm.

And so he too entered into the peace and quiet the outdoors provided.

I will become a branch in the breeze.
All was calm.

He stashed the blood soaked wad of green paper dollars in his front jeans pocket. He had seventy-five cents in the same pocket before he entered the house. He was going to get a medium coffee from the seven eleven before he saw the light … but now with his recent windfall he might get a Clearly Canadian and a sandwich, potato salad too if they have any fresh made.

No turning back now, aye.

After this they would come looking for him.

His only real hope was to go on the lam and cross the boarder into canada.

A flight to freedom.

He'd have to move west a bit to downplay any suspicion.
It would be a hike but he could hitch for some of it.
He had a book at home that detailed Tubman's underground railroad.

He could use this to avoid the authorities for a while, he had a plan.

The sun warmed his back as he walked casting his large shadow across the lawns of the neighborhood. Children played with water pistols while the grey housing slumped in august heat. He passed a white haired man lounging in a chair watering a tropical green lawn. The man politely waved.

He might have been neighborhood watch checking out the new face.

It was always polite when wearing a hat, to tip ones hat in respect to ones elders.

He pulled a hand from his jeans pocket and tipped his hat and kept moving casually down the sidewalk.

He came to the corner, looked both ways and crossed the street with very little regard for the opposite light being green

.

Even with a hat on sweat managed to run down his cheek. He wiped at his face a few times until he finally took his hat off completely ran a hand across his brow. It was hot for august, this kind of heat drives anyone to extremes. He had to go north to cool off. The heat was making him crazy. The answer lay up north somewhere; somewhere north to cool off. Skip saw the seven eleven sign poking out through the maple trees near end of the long row of houses. He would get a ham sandwich and a raspberry cooler. It's five blocks to freedom, his own fortress of solitude. He would be back in his room with a ham sandwich and from there who knows?

But wait

Look up in the sky

it's a bird

its a plane

no
its
its Superman

Faster than a
speeding Bullet

more powerful than a
locomotive

able to leap tall buildings in a
single bound

its Superman

Canto 39

Vishnu

Perhaps the highest of the Hindu gods,

the personification of the preserving power of the divine spirit.
blue in color
with his four hands he holds
a shell
a quoit
a club
a lotus
Vishnu rests on the serpent of eternity

Vishnu appears in many incarnations as the messenger
vivid aspects of the god in earthly quantities

In the Hindu mythos the Avatars of Vishnu are many

Matsya
as a fish came to the good king Satyavrate
instructing him to built a great ark
for   he and his family
the beasts of the earth
the birds of the sky
and
seven sages
all escaped the terrible flood
that swamped the worlds wickedness

Kurma
the tortoise
supporting
Mount Mandara on his back
while the gods churn the sea for ambrosia

Varaha
appeared as a boar
going into the sea
fishing out the Earth
on its tusks
the second time the Earth drowned

Narasingha
the man lion   saved the world from the monarch
endowed with universal dominion
by the gods.

Krishna

Born from a hair of Vishnu
he placed in the womb of Devaki

Krishna was exchanged for the newborn daughter
of Nanda, and his wife Yasoda
Devaki was instructed by Kansa that her son would seize control

and so it was Krishna who went on his journey

slay the serpent Kaliya,
abduct the daughter of the Gandharva king,
overthrow the flying city of Daityas,
and obtain the discus from the fire god Agni.

On reaching manhood,
Krishna left the cowherds and returned to Mathura,

here he killed Kansa
as was foretold in prophecy

He was central
in the war of

Pandavas and the Kauravas

the hunter Jaras felled Krishna with his arrow
and Krishna was dead

Buddha is said to have been an Avatar of Vishnu …

Nine of these Avatars have come to pass

the tenth is to be called Kalki Avatara
he will appear
armed with a scimitar
riding a white horse
he will end the present age
to inaugurate the new world

Nine of these Avatars have come to pass

the tenth is to be called Kalki Avatara
he will appear
the tenth is to be called Kalki Avatara
he will appear
the tenth is to be called Kalki Avatara
he will appear

armed with a scimitar
riding a white horse
he will end the present age

to inaugurate the new world

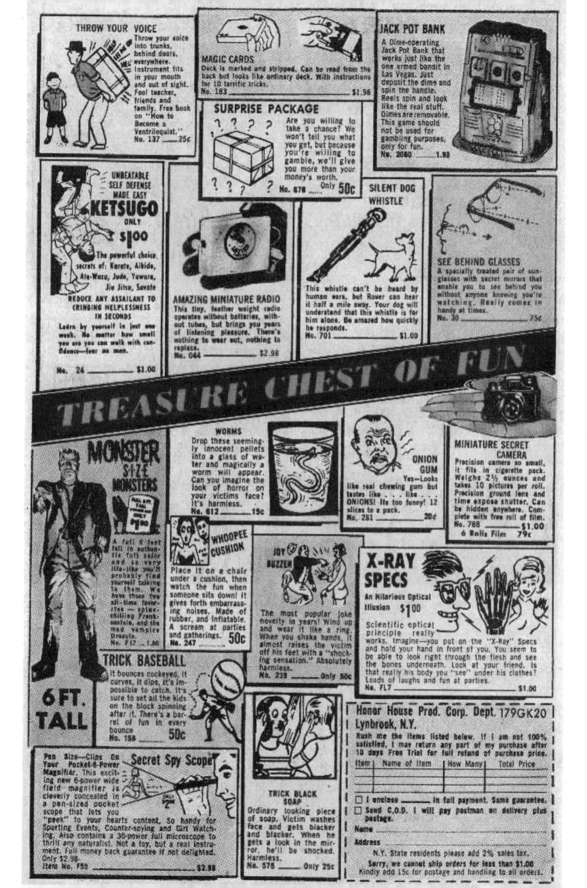

Canto 40

In March 1938, Siegel and Shuster sell the first *Superman* story for $10 per page and all rights to their character Superman to DC Comics for $130. They were unable to sell their story into newspaper syndication. The sample Superman newspaper strips were rejected by United Features Syndicate, Esquire Features, and Bell Syndicate. *Action Comics* #1 debuted in June 1938 introducing Superman/Clark Kent and fellow reporter Lois Lane at the *Daily Star* newspaper (later renamed by the radio show to *Daily Planet* in 1940), with a first run of 200,000 copies priced at 10 cents. It would be selling 500,000 copies monthly by issue #7. It was in 1940 Siegel and Shuster begin to think that they made an unwise business decision.

The son of the Kryptonian scientist Jor-El and his wife Lara,

they named him Kal-El

Superman was born in the Kryptonian capital Kryptonopolis
in the earth calendar month of October in the year 1920

bearing an unmistakable resemblance to his father

The House of El,
a heritage of achievement
            this boy was born to do great things
in the fields of science, statesmanship, and exploration

An ancestry teeming of lasting distinction
Val-El, an explorer and discoverer
Sul-El, the inventor of Krypton's first telescope
Tala-El, the author of Krypton's planet-wide constitution
Hatu-El, a scientist and inventor
Gam-El, the father of modern Kryptonian architecture

Superman was still when his planet exploded
            shining green fragments
a cataclysmic chain reaction of the planet's molten core

A Superman among men, among the universes many colored beings

his parents had placed him in an experimental rocket ship
launching him toward the warmth of the planet Earth
There Kal-El, who would one day be known throughout the universe

world-famous crime-fighter adventurer masking his true identity beneath a mild-mannered guise his alter ego, journalist Clark Kent, is the hero Superman veteran adventurer	is in one sense a man of two men	Kal-el the world's mightiest hero, ally of Batman, the cousin of Supergirl, owner of Krypto the Superdog, is also Clark Kent, mild-mannered journalist,

On Sunday's Jonathan Kent takes his wife Martha for a drive
In Smallville
in 1923
this is luxury
Having no children of their own they could afford a car
Martha wanted children but was never able to carry after

She miscarried once and never got over it

From heavens wishing orphaned from a doomed planet a rocket had crossed the universe bringing to safety bringing to Earth bringing to Martha a son landing in an open field on the outskirts of Smallville.	Martha screamed at the fire streaking across the evening sky The autumn skies burned the night Jonathan, watching the streaking star travel, swerved the car

Martha screamed as they crashed into a side ditch, tire flat the rocket crashed near by	Jonathan, watched the star open, like an egg for a boy to emerge	wrapped in a glory red cloth a golden crest of a diamond S two fingers together pointing towards heaven

The proud new parents embraced their a new son Jonathan baptized as Clark, Martha Kent's maiden name	The Kent's sold their farm moved to Smallville where Jonathan opened a general store

the name of Clark Kent means integrity and honesty.

Clark Kent alters his appearance with eye-glasses
exhibits personal qualities far different than those of Superman

As Clark Kent
a persona enabled

can catch the criminal element unaware
can safeguard his friends against terrific reprisals

affords him a refuge
making possible for him an escape

to relate to ordinary work a day folk on everyday human terms	Clark Kent is meek, mild-mannered, sickly, weak, submissive, and is even considered spineless by Lois Lane

is afraid of dogs, is afraid of heights, and is willing to let almost anyone push him around.	Taking cues from the Scarlet Pimpernel "My meek behavior is the *perfect disguise* for my real identity as *Superman*!"	Clark Kent is over 30 years of age has black hair and blue eyes the muscular figure of that generations ideal of magnificent symmetry and physique The finest physical specimen 6'2" tall, chest measurement of 44" waist measurement of 34"

while having a unique atomic structure	Clark Kent is widely known as Superman's best friend to contact Kent at the *Daily Planet* is to touch Superman

Clark Kent attended Metropolis High School was nicknamed "Specs" became known as class's quietest boy.	**[OR]**	Clark Kent grew up in Smallville, attended Smallville High School working afternoons in his father's store. Seen as the shyest boy in his graduating class, his senior class yearbook: "highest grades - boy most likely to become famous"

Clark Kent attended Metropolis University He lived in a dormitory, joined a fraternity, yelled his heart out as a cheerleader for the home team.	had already decided upon a career in journalism

Nevertheless, he studied advanced science taking courses in biology, astronomy, art, music, and other liberal art subjects	Clark Kent as a reporter for a major newspaper investigates criminals without suspecting that he's really Superman provides him opportunities to help people as Superman without explanations	"As a reporter," notes Kent in December, 1949, "I have a hundred underworld and police contacts that make it easier for Superman to fight crime!"

Clark Kent is renowned for his ability to root out a story, crime, corruption, war correspondent, editor in the absence of Perry White	Clark Kent in pursuit of a story goes under cover a detective, a fireman, and a policeman he has joined the Marines; he has become a bum on the skids. a police commissioner, a department store clerk, a sheriff, a vacuum cleaner salesman, and a disc jockey. He has even gone to prison to investigate a series of prison riots to learn where a hardened convict hid his stolen loot.

Martha Kent urged Clark to hide his wonderful gifts until the time came
But Mother when? He would ask.

Jonathan furrowed his brow, Now listen to me, Clark, listen with your heart
you have a strength that will frighten people. This is natural as people will not understand
you are not from this world and people do not understand what they do not know
you've got to hide it from people or they'll be scared of you.

But when the proper time comes, his mother beamed, you must use it to assist humanity
to help all those who you can

But I am not human, would this not be out of balance

Clark, listen with your heart follow that path and only that path as the events of today dictate a history the actions of today build the person of tomorrow	Superman was not always famous In the early days he sought anonymity newspaper accounts omitted mention him

many of people he encountered expressed surprise

a legendary character
people doubted Superman's existence

It was the 3rd day when Clark Kent was called home to attend the wedding of Lana Lang	the daughter of archaeologist and explorer Professor Lang and niece of Professor Potter, grew up in Smallville, where she was in Clark Kent's class at Smallville High School

Clark loved her as only a boy can
the object of her was desire, she was all things sweet
shining as all things that the mind adores shines

She did not love him as he loved her she was taken aback, that uncomfortable feeling of love born in the heart and not of the head As was her nature, she understood and was kind she suspected something wondrous in Clark behind those glasses but he would never let her see in Clark Kent sat with his mother at the reception table	After the cake was served and band called for dancing Clark remember that he had left his present, a 2 slice toaster, in the trunk of their green sedan, excusing himself politely he sat in the front seat of the car with a longing heart the radio played Gershwin as he watched the bride kiss her new husband with his super vision

"We interrupt this broadcast to bring you a news flash	**Flash,**	A meteor was just spotted in Earth's upper outer atmosphere. Reports coming in from the Metropolis observatory projects its impact in a matter of minutes … Its heading unknown

Up Up and Away	a streak of red an blue arcs up towards the black horizons

up towards iron melting
bracing against the atmosphere

he see it immediately if he had not let his guard down there would be more time if he punches it there it will shard if he catches it the shock will shatter in a spray	must redirect it NOW and with a flip in flight under, up and out

Superman flies into the meteor and braces
the flying metal ore against his back
his red cape fluttering

And now to push you back off to space
where you will not harm anyone

Superman shifts its flight path with an oomph
the meteor sails the vast distance of open space

But wait,
 	
   a chunk had broken
away heading for Smallville
heading right for the wedding
reception
        must hurry
	It was a race against time
	must warn the people
	must catch the iron ore
		
		only seconds to
		spare

It was a time to act
and Superman flew in action
through the front doors and floated above the dancing wedding crowd
Professor Potter pointed "Look up in the Sky"
      "People, you must take shelter now
        there is a meteor …

panic overtook the crowd,
what, from where, who are
"People you must …"

what, from where, who are
And it is Martha Kent who calls to her friends
"Whatsoever he says to you, do it"

"People, you must take shelter now.
I will stop the danger but it is heading for this spot ….

And the wedding party fled from the building, still not wondering

still pondering true

When with a crash they could see the distant star coming closer

This strange man told the truth, they were in danger and all looked bleak

Lana hid in her Husband arms for what seemed the last time
how could she die on this day of all days, who was that man

how could he fly, he was handsome, how could he save them

were the questions of the crowd as they followed the red blue streak fly to meet the danger head on.
Who was this brave soul and how did he come to this day?

And Superman flew

they both impacted the Earth
Smallville was safe again
Superman flew up and circled in the sky

And Superman flew

into the falling star
falling
falling away from the gathering
falling away into a field miles from any living

Later : at the bandstand podium, the mayor, the bride, and the hero stood

At every wedding that I have been to
in the past
at the beginning of a meal good wine
is set out;
and when men have drank enough
to dull their senses,
that is when the lesser quality brand
is poured:

But this day I have ordered up the
finest wine
and we shall drink a toast to this day

a day that will stay with us for a long
time
a feasting of the marriage of our
towns finest daughters
and the coming of a new hero to our
town

Superman, I present you with
the key to the city of Smallville

and offer to you the goodwill
of the people you have this
day saved

manifesting
goodwill
and glory
among the
people

and so after this day
the people believed on him

Canto 41

the globe on top of the
Daily Planet
spins over metropolis

We can see the bend of
the earths curve from this
height

into distance

there seems to be
too many stars in the sky

pieces too close
closer than the moon
coming

The City is Dark
orange outlines black skylines

electricity has gone out in times like this
the people are frightened

There is a sedan upturned
engine on fire

This too before

coming across the heavens

chunks

of

iron

ore

off course from the Oort Cloud
on the rim of our solar system

coming in

The scientists
on their telescopes

just now saw them

I am glad I could help

like I have a
choice

The caped figure
flies head first,
hands dive into,
at the, heart
of the largest of
the flaming
meteors

there are
hundreds

As it explodes he flies through the ruin

hitting another
running into its course
hitting another

to divide the storm
hitting another

hitting another

bringing order back to the skies

but wait!
off in the distance
a cargo ship is in trouble

one of the meteors fell in the ocean

if he did nothing
the wake would sunder the ship.

Over his head in one arm

he flies into port with the broken ship

twisted metal   men on the deck cheering   to the crowds at shore

the man of steel saves the American day

Again; takes flight

one fist is poised out
        front
his other is by his side
        ready

furrowed brow
a determined eye
lips grimace
a curl of hair in the front

red cape flusters high in the wind

A man with a thick
mustache

waves his green ball cap

to the red image taking
flight
there is hope in an empty
cold world

his other hand holds a
wrench

There is a difference in having ability and using ability	to one it is not worth having the other presupposes you know how the right method in which to use In any case you don't win. If you do nothing it is everything to do everything becomes no choice	it wasn't easy to come to this I was in Smallville; a hurt friend no help anywhere we flew to the hospital

if you have a gun people will ask you to shoot at things for them if you can ease pain the pained will seek you out

is there really an obligation	or am I just too soft inside and if you miss even one …

victims have criticisms too and they are sirens the greater good applies only to textbooks essays in crisis it is the self mourning the self that has lost	His ears can pick up many distance sounds	the story they once resided in with inside the mind there is a narrative an abstraction placed over the promise of future days that never happen but are dreamed and transacted within the self around the self and for the dreamers dreams he lies near

This reminds me I have a dinner planned with Lois	She will know where I am a modernist's ideal of a hard nosed reporter too tough for her own good. hates it when I am late for a date she is always in control she needs to win she feels conflict if she is not on the right side	He punches things when they are close enough He rams through solid rock, a needle through cloth He kicks through metal walls

long straight black hair
business suit and skirt
                white pearls
a hat when in fashion
anyone beneath her cannot get close
she has a heart of gold
I love her
she, strangely loved me as object
but found herself open to the real

I love her

He punches things when they are close enough
He rams through solid rock, a needle through cloth
He kicks through metal walls

he is aggressive

                                    but
measures his

                                    weight
against

and cause further

so as to not
overwhelm

                                    he has
learned this the
hard way

all current success is informed by failure

even supermen fail

in arctic waste he finds comfort

Fortress of Solitude, his secret sanctuary	from an unrelenting battle against the forces of evil and injustice, he takes a moment to reflect the day and leave it here before

Clark Kent is over 30 years of age
has black hair and blue eyes
the muscular figure of that generations ideal of magnificent symmetry and physique

The finest physical specimen
6'2" tall,
chest measurement of 44"
waist measurement of 34"

there were other romantic involvements
fascinating women as Lana Lang, Lori Lemaris, Lyla Lerrol, and Sally Selwyn.

But tonight it is Lois Lane he is having dinner with. Not as Superman But as Superman in his relaxed bowtie These things once confused him believing people would understand that he was different and still wanted to have a life To have and have not defines every soul under a yellow sun	The party was for friends and family, and Clark was neither, but as a guest of Lois he managed to just make the reception. She "He's off covering that Superman story" "His friend isn't he" "Yes I read that interview he did just after that Luthor incident" "Oh there's Clark now …"
They embrace he smells of ice and smoke She has never been more happy to see him	Even though this same thing happened yesterday. This is why she loves him he defies what he should ; is for her

Ah Clark, how is our favorite friend? a hand ruffles his hair	We were just commenting on how there is no more wine and how the whole party would be saved if you would be kind enough to fly down to the shop and pick us up some thing red.	well get the glasses ready I'll be right back and out he walks
And Lois carried on, clapping her hands once and the host nods to the waitress and the glasses were brought	in a flash of blue crosses the globe	And in he walks within seconds of leaving carrying in three cases of French wine. I was donating this to a charity banquet, it's a very nice blend from our cellars, I hope this will do ….
Hands on the back the band plays on the party is only beginning not saved who do you think I am ? Cheers to the beautiful union of two souls lucky enough to find themselves in love and together. It is a large universe a glass raises		in the corner alone a man seethes
The Next Day: The offices of the Daily Planet are always rifling typewritten copy fluttering in the air gestures of rapid production		Jimmy Olsen: Hey get a load of this *pointing to a magazine* Perry White: I can't believe Superman would do such a thing. Lois Lane: Clark take a look at this Clark Kent: Oh my

A DaDa-cola advertising Superman quenching his super thirst on a water-tower filled with DaDa-cola spilling into his Super mouth. He looks like he likes it too. There is something in his printed eye that says its all American to drink DaDa-cola and if Superman drinks DaDa-cola you should too. Its Super cool to be in with DaDa-cola.

Even Superman winks to this notion

Lois Lane: Clark what do you …

Clark Kent's not there anymore, only his whooshing trail of a suit

leading to an open window

Superman flew past a billboard being pasted up at the Metropolis baseball stadium

he made a scourge of small cords

He swung his scourge

He could never condone this

He swung his scourge

A man in white overalls and painters cap looked stunned. His glue brush had glued that billboard straight up.

Does he complain to his union?

He was more afraid of Superman than his foreman at the moment.
His thermos tipped over.

Superman: Who told you to do this?

Man: I just work for the stadium, Mr. Super, or is it Mr. Man. I … don't hurt me!

Superman : I wouldn't hurt you. You do not have permission over my image, but that hardly calls for ...

whites doves overhead

For the very first time, he confronts the evil that had escaped him all this time. He Didn't mind generating for charity,
but DaDa-cola doesn't need help to sell

Sell my face not to a house of merchandise

Corporate Housing of DaDa-cola, Atlanta, Ga.

In through the window flies the Man of Steel The marketing executives all look up in a daze. *Pointing*, Superman : Your zeal to sell your soft drinks has eaten me up. Why would you do this without my permission?	Jordan Almond: I gave the green light on that Superman. I looked you up and you don't have any rights on the image of yourself, only the self in which you are. Superman : I have rights just as you have rights. I own this body and the likenesses of it and should have just say in such matters as any citizen

After a long pause Superman sits down in a black leather seat at the head board room table. The other executives take notice and do the same. Jordan Almond sits off to the right.

Superman : If you use my image you use my self. You have the power to influence just as I have the power to inspire as well as this can promote the insipid in us all

This all comes from a greater sense of duty to something beyond making that bonus, but doing real good for real people, and although entertainment is refreshing ….

If you destroy this image I have built up over the years of service I have performed	To break down the trust of the American people only to sell a soft drink is to cheapen the wants and needs of the people who are frightened	The want to have the power to overcome the situation they are facing and the need to overcome it with dignity with stride
I will rebuild it in 3 issues but he was not talking about his narrative	They read me only to comfort the real terror they live in day in and day out, be that mental or physical	To have a power the likes of the powers written within me is to call upon the greatest of man's desires. To fly unhampered by strings, to fix what is broken, to see beyond the molecular level, all things within the form of one person who's singular want is to alleviate suffering

The marketing executives agreed that he was an image of goodwill but who had the right to control the want of the people who needed something of this honor to hold onto. Was he that erudite as to dismiss the common man from expressing their support through the only voice they trust .

Jordan Almond : That being merchandise. One could question your intent and endorsement of the American flag to that of Ralph Loren in his Polo line of clothes.

you know that

this is different

is this not America

And DaDa-cola stopped the campaigns
as they came to know that he was for all men and not
And needed not that any should testify of man

And when Superman stopped Doomsday
Jordan Almond remembered this meeting
for he knew what was in man

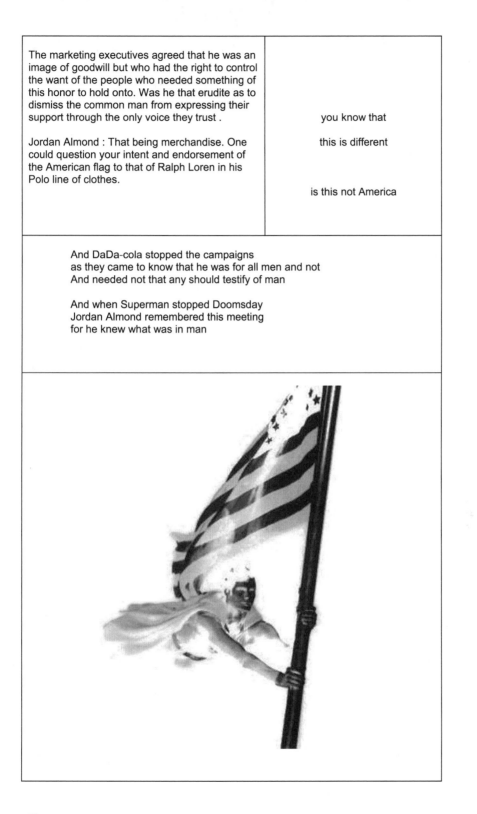

Canto 42

Behind lies a star
an emerald veil the glimmer of a star

> A green man
> A bowler
> A white boutonniere
> A plaid bowtie

A bald man his deep green

> suit lifts his bald head from the glass countertop
> of Max's deli
next to grain mustards and napkins
Straws and a front page of today's Planet

Of course its Kosher, Max says, I even use Iceberg lettuce

> Max chugs a laughs and slaps the counter
> the man in green looks up from his sandwich
> wipes his mouth

So I see Superman nabbed the South end Seven.
Bank robbers them. It was round the corner at the First national …

> Super Jerk! again!
> my favorite game

I beg your pardon … Max stuttered outwardly looking for a

> name

> Nick. Just go with Nick.
> My name is unpronounceable here.

My parents changed their name coming over too.
As if Shlomo Johnson is more american
> he says into the wind or their spirit

But wait, this is no ordinary customer in Max's Deli

This is the Fifth Dimensional being Mr. Mxyzptlk
(pronounced mit-yez-pittle-ick) who sole purpose is annoy
a devilish being from another plane of reality,
different in every way from our own,
a place he calls

a fifth dimension

The trickster Loki
Another coyote
whose deviousness knows no bounds or limits,
Using his amazing scientific skills he can manipulate
Earthly matter in a manner that appears magical.

deciding on a challenge and a condition to determine when he'll leave,
generally this wagers on him recognizing his name in reversed

His past includes
                    forcing Superman and the Flash to compete against one
                    another in an around-the-world foot race,

                    the creation of Red Kryptonite,
                              a variant version more deadly than
                              green Kryptonite temporarily robbing
                              Superman
                              of his powers.

            Ever unpredictable,
            Mxyzptlk continues
            to plot and scheme,

            waiting for his next mission
            waiting for a mission of mayhem.

)

Mxyzptlk turns from the lunch counter
sandwich in hand newspaper in the other
and pushes his way out the door,
the bell ringing, with another hand

                  Max hears the bell
                  turns

                              HEY
                              you didn't pay

                  Up and Over the counter
                  Max follows

Mxyzptlk wrapped in his own thoughts and grins
sees an angry Max charging at him

his small form leaps catlike and meets him in mid air
                    they hit
                    Mxyzptlk lands on top
                    he pulls another hand

            his fingers form gun-like
            No not a gun, it's a flower
a white flower aimed at Max's head,
prone   the petals tickle

                        is this death
                        is this the end

from a flower?

Now how can I teach you about inter   dimension spatial relations
        when you don't even understand earthly relations?

        is this the end, indeed
                        A flower can't hurt you Maxy
                        and with a sandwich like yours
        we know that you are a teacher come directly from god himself

                a pop
                he was gone
                $10 in Max's front pocket with a post it note

                Stating : What goes quack at the noon time bell?

        Max scratches his head
        then as the hour turns
        so did he, into a large yellow duck

Later that Day in the newsroom of the Daily Planet

It was two pm now and the article had to be in by three
A follow up on the South end Seven, to put a face on crime
the criminals and their families – why they stole was more
interesting than their capture. Well at least to Clark Kent.

Five men two women one family and three banks
The mother was ill, another operation needed.
When the plant closed Dr. Tableau offered no more credit
There was nothing more to do, his wife wouldn't hear of it

So to the banks they went and through their efforts
would afford the finest unmarried doctor in Metropolis
and maybe even take a trip, but then Superman
ruined everything, arrested them all, danger was healed

Superman gave help to the mother too
finding some proper care and a nurse
to take her pain from her now empty home
it is a sad story it should sell well

The telephone rings
Clark lets it go

A voice from behind, are you going to answer that?
        Would you take it Jimmy, I have to finish … then

A package for Mr. Kent
resounds through the busy newsroom
typers stop typing and copyboys went green marking time.

        But Kent keeps to his work

[BANG]

      and still nothing from Kent

What do I have to do to get your attention? I stop time, I blow up the office, I even bring you a cheesecake and you love cheese cake.

      I heard from Max, I knew you were coming Mxyzptlk

That's a fine sandwich he makes, I travel across dimensions especially for him, and well for you too

      Why don't you come back at a better time?
      I could schedule you in for tomorrow …

I could take your friend here and make him into a rocket
launch it towards Moscow so he too could be from above

      Haven't I saved him from something similar before?
      Nothing that goes up does not come back down.

      With all your knowledge your science
      this is the path you choose, why?

Only when evenly matched should one fight?
What fun is that? You save and you never play

      To be truly enlightened one must come from the wind

From the makeup of these stunning cities of stars is to me a music that launches into being all things But with you, we are of the same we are both enamored by these simple people

But we don't need them. They are flesh and we are of what they call a spirit realm
Come and play I'll be the cat this time, no kryptonite I promise. What do you say?

      But Kent had not once looked up from his Remington typewriter
      a sign that discourse was not to be transacted upon, a hard return

So you'd prefer going around judging
then turning a dollar on their hardships
this is what tedium yours parents saved you for

There was nothing more my father could do for Krypton
      he knew of this planet and I did not have to die there,
           and so I was sent here, not to judge or be judged, but to help

          if anyone believes in me, my role is fulfilled. I am
          a small character as are you

Oh you're a character all right what are you writing

      Stop lurking in the darkness come into the light and
      read what this is about

      And Kent hands him a paper

and pop the newsroom was back in a fluster
he was gone and the paper flutters to the ground :

kltpzyxm kltpzyxm kltpzyxm kltpzyxm kltpzyxm kltpzyxm kltpzyxm
kltpzyxm kltpzyxm kltpzyxm kltpzyxm kltpzyxm kltpzyxm kltpzyxm kltpzyxm
kltpzyxm kltpzyxm kltpzyxm kltpzyxm kltpzyxm kltpzyxm kltpzyxm kltpzyxm

The other side of town

The paper arrived at 5 PM exactly
the man dressed for dinner standing at the door
reached out and caught the toss from the boy on the red flyer

It was the home of David Blaine
millionaire and crime fighter
Captain Avenger; and his helper Bucky

opened the paper and folded it distinctly and threw it in the fire

What is it about him that attracts so many?
we used to have the headlines before he showed up

Oh Bucky, don't be this way
I told you that we would fade

But we saved a family from a burning building last night
and that's on page three, captured a kidnapper last month – that made the
paper weeks later

One can only have what is given to them.
Don't we do this for reasons better than media's kiss?

We were his forerunner, and for that we should act in concert

Any person who believes in a superhero is our friend
and that one who
chooses to prey one the weak shall be his to tend to,
and if he misses then our wrath shall rest upon him

SMOKING *is for* SQUARES!

PUBLISHED AS A PUBLIC SERVICE IN COOPERATION WITH THE NATIONAL SOCIAL WELFARE ASSEMBLY, COORDINATING ORGANIZATION FOR NATIONAL HEALTH, WELFARE AND RECREATION AGENCIES OF THE U.S.

Canto 43

For Shawn Kelly
'Every time a bell rings an angel gets his wings'
Zuzu Bailey

Eisenhower Supreme Allied Commander
RADAR
Count Fleet wins the triple crown

I may make you feel but I can't make you think.
    a memory, a flute

    And so, recalls Clark Kent years later,
    "soon, under the sea, we kissed
    there never was, or ever will be,
    such a strange kiss again
    the farewell kiss between a Superman and a mermaid!

    Superman is said to derive powers, in part, from the ultra solar rays
    of Earth's yellow sun, and the gradual evolution of decades of texts
    extraordinary magnifications of ordinary human ability

    While you can toss a baseball,
    he can launch an entire planet

the ordinary man
    can see across the street,
    he can see across creation.

      When Supergirl first came to earth and found Superman,
          he explained
      we would not be super-powered, even under low gravity

    only yellow stars emit super energy rays
    These rays affect people born in solar systems other than Earth's

    On Planets of non-yellow suns,

    we are vulnerable

Once
this man could leap 1/8th of a mile, hurdle a twenty-story building,
raise tremendous weights, run faster than an express train,
nothing less than a bursting shell could penetrate his skin

    once he could not fly

Today
Superman can withstand the heat at the core of the sun,

soar through the air at a speed thousands of times the speed of light,

extinguish a star with a puff of his breath as though it was only a scented candle
Incredible? No! For even today on our world exist creatures with super-strength!

There is a lovely brown-haired Atlantean mermaid,
                    Her name, Lori Lemaris,
            the kind of girl he's always dreamed of marrying
                    an unconventional beauty
                            in her eyes burned blue mystery

                        She was seated in a wheel chair
                        a plaid throw covered her legs

            But this all happened years ago,
            when he was studying at Metropolis U,
            seeing what this world could offer

They met careening down a hill on the campus lawn

            She was in danger, quick to act, but could not be overt as Kent

Focusing the heat of his X-ray vision he melted the rubber of the wheels
This way he could run at a normal speed to catch the woman in distress
the wheels stopped, jerked, and let her fly up, up and into Kent's arms

            The shock vanished
            when she looked up
            saw Clark, as hero and smiled

            Oh my chair, it it … thank you

            He was taken with her immediately
            Her desire for life alongside disability

            And that beautiful face, and a feeling

            It felt like she was looking into my mind

            then she was off and Clark to Class

She was on his mind through out his Biology lesson
Lori Lemaris, a lovely name for a lovely woman

It was the next week before Clark found her
sitting at a dark wooden table in the library

She was reading a book on US Soviet relations
drinking from a large bottle of water, Clark walked over

                    May I have a drink of your water? he stammered

Lori looked up and coolly stated,

But you don't even have a glass

But its VivaAquae, my favorite brand
who ever drinks from this shall never thirst again
Ba ba da bada ba dada ba, he finishes the jingle

She giggles,   I'd pay a million for that if it was real,

Well, I'll settle for half in cash, now

Mr. Kent that would be super of you,

He stops. Wait a minute, he thinks.
There's no way that she could know that I am superman.

A well of sensation began springing up, fear or maybe everlasting love
she knew so much about him from the moment they fell into one another

They dated steadily for the next semester
while
she insisting on always being home by 8

Clark was graduating in Spring
Having an internship at the Daily Planet he felt ready to begin a career

He was also asking himself if he was ready to go forward,
alone
He loved Lori and wanted to open his life to a woman and marriage
but the threat to anyone close to Superman
was to great to ask anyone to join

He would have to hang up the cape,
do the vacuuming when her parents came into town
become ordinary

But for Lori Lemaris
his heart told him it was right

So months went blissfully by for Clark and Lori
Parties, movies, exams, parades and rallies rolled on in their love

when the time came Clark make his offer he flew
to the mountains of Africa and mined the perfect diamond,
large as it was, it still managed to fit on a delicate ring of gold

There was a moon out
and Superman flew to her
ring in hand, orchids from Tahiti

And then knocked as gentile as Clark would
Lori answered the door, Clark what are you …

Clark?
How long have you known,
How could you …

Its so obvious isn't it, twisting her hands in her blanketed lap

Did you think you could hide anything in our love?

Then will you marry me?
Kneeling before her chair, red fluttered
She cradled the flowers and he opened the velvet box

She glowed before the ring and the life it held

Clark, if that is what I should call you

That's my name, on earth, it's also Kal-el.
Marry me Lori I love you

Oh Clark this is wonderful, but I cannot
please come in, she said rolling backwards

I there someone else?
If the outfit is over the top I can …

Of course not silly,
as you have hid from me I too hide a secret from you.

Lori waited a moment, then with a swift yank
lifted her blanketed legs. But they were not legs
they were scales, no a fin, and it all came clear

This lovely brown-haired woman
seated in a wheel chair
a plaid throw covered her legs

Her name, Lori Lemaris,
the kind of girl he's always dreamed of marrying
an unconventional beauty
in her eyes burned blue mystery

Atlantean mermaid, Lori Lemaris,
the kind of girl he's always dreamed of marrying

Superman gaped.
He had never even considered this
Of all things he imagined
(the most extreme to discover a way for her to walk)
her being a mermaid was totally new

I cannot marry you because I have come to the surface for only a
year and must return to the deep. I owe my people as much as
you to your world.

I am a descendant of Nar Lemaris, the Atlantean scientist who
performed the miraculous biological conversion that transformed
the people of Atlantis into a population of mer-people; soon I am
to be ruler of Atlantis.

I cannot be away from salt water for very long. This is why I come
home so early from our dates. Do you understand? Please tell
me you understand. The last thing I want is to hurt you. Yes, I
love you. I have loved you from far, even before I fell.

And you knew about my secret identity how?
Did you see my cape under my oxford shirt?

Well we had to adapt for underwater communications
There was no speaking. We became telepaths,
and in your arms one night I sought your mind

and there it was, I told no one, and you will tell no one of me?

Superman, of course, nodded and was quite graceful indeed
They flew off to together towards the south seas and swam
as they knew this would be one of their last moments
dancing under the crystal waters
in love

she promised to inform all of Atlantis
that he is an ally and a truly super man

In the coming days before graduation,
after saying his good byes to Lori
Clark remained in his fraternity house

His frat brothers came to him noticing that he had missed meals for a week
Clark, you have to eat sometime. Come on out and be a man.

Oh, I am man and I have meat to chew on that you know nothing of. He winked.

Who brought Clark food? They joked. No really who here has brought anything
to 'down in the dumps' Kent lately? Hmmn. I see. You have been locked up here
listening to that radio and making a spectacle of yourself. Clark, we are worried and want to
help.

Thank you he replied. I grew up on a farm and I fall back into thinking off alone

There are still four months to harvest time.
I tell you, Lift up your eyes, and look on the fields;
they are white and now already to harvest.

On the old Kent farm back in Smallville
you go out and work all day in the heat,
and dirt wearing gloves for days wages

Dad used to quote to me

he that reapeth receiveth wages, and gathereth fruit unto life eternal:
that both he that soweth and he that reapeth may rejoice together.

I guess that that means to me all things come to a circle of joy,
or working in cycles to come together always for harvest.
Not living with the beginnings of hope in seeds and hay
and dreams and the possible ends but in the mean while
concentrating on the moment you are in flux. Act on wit.

One sows what another man reaps while both enjoy autumn

Whatever Clark, just eat something

I don't want to leave her now

I know I don't even know how

        I don't know
        I don't know

Something in the way she knows, all I have to do is just think of her

        I don't know
        It's just no good

then,
A brake from the radio: Flash –

        tonight fire rages over the Vector factory in the west end we have
        crews going to the scene as we speak,. This station will keep you
        informed of any late breaking news;

from the blackened rooftops Clark would see the blaze, he felt his heart

looking left towards the closet where he hung up this blue suit
Then right towards the blaze
and down to the floor boards

        Moments later Superman
        takes flight, whooshes past
        the factory and with him

        blows out the fire in one
        deep
        breath

        he does not stop
        continuing around the globe

        hoping something would break

        Nothing did, and nothing would he slowed down and flew into an
open window of the Daily Planet building, quickly changing, rushes towards the newsroom

    Kent get over here now, it was Perry White, acting editor, we have a fire over at
Vector and no one here to cover it. I need you to run

    I was just there. Its out. Superman came by and …

        Great Caesar's ghost!

    Sir?

        Do you think you can write it up for the next run …
        in say twenty minutes

    You need me to perform tricks and wonders to make you see me seriously as a real
reporter?

Kent I'll remind you that you are the intern around here,
can you do it or not -- If you do you'll have a fulltime job

If you believe in me then, I will have it for you by 1

This is again the second sign
that Superman did that evening

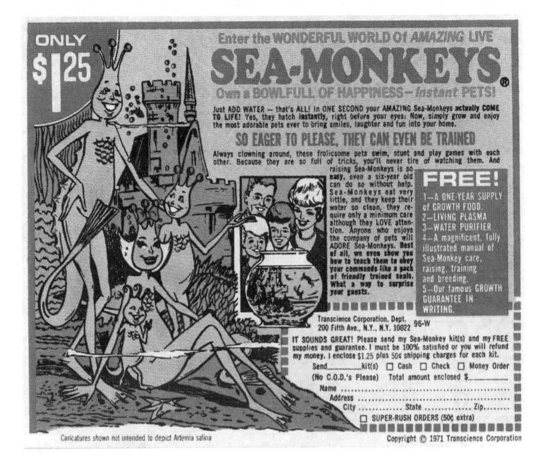

Canto 44

The Normandy invasion D-Day
Hitler introduces rockets
Battle of the Bulge
Glenn Miller disappears
GI Joe and Sad Sack appear

He is a lonely scientist working in his white lab coat
Pocket of pens and a slide rule leans by his right arm
A white lab and a grey Bunsen burner burning brite

Never believe it's not so

triangle beakers and bottles red and blue,
a yellow graduated measure boils liquor
A chalk board marks time sliding away

His dinner was cold two hours ago
his wife or his child will cover it
he cannot come home this time

The work is not as important as it is precise
He will never reach engineering prominence
He publishes papers to retain his annual raise

I feel quite alone these days in defending

Never believe it's not so

What interests me more is the flight
from power that persists my profession,

some of whom began with an innate ability
to experience the electrical value but today
Strength alone can open it up,
persistent cognitive negations

Have produced for the first time
the power source needed for my
Robot to move. Thunder clap clap

A black blue frame set apart in the right hand corner
White streaks thin then thick, Clap Clap boom
Thunder underscores the black intent of Science over man

Never believe it's not so

In Freud, flight is the metaphor for repression,
for unconscious yet purposeful forgetting.

In the Man of Steel, it is freedom purchased
by obligations of what to do and what could

In Science, it is unattainable cognitive negation

76

over what could be done if only they understood

     The purpose is clear enough
     Never believe it's not so

displaced guilt with an unending power source
The Robot will show both the power of science
as well the benefits of the ordinary man's work

but they would have been thinking of the same story
the creation of life from falsified means. No birth
experience upon the heights. Those who descend from there,

     chant the chorus
     a mystification advanced
          Never believe it's not so

Bethesda, Maryland
Annual Conference for Scientific Advancement

Gee Mister Kent why did The Planet send us down here?

To hear the paper on the new power source Jimmy.
Its going to revolutionize the way we move around

Well as long as we stop at the one eyed alligator exhibit it will be a trip worthwhile.

Just make sure you have your camera ready for this

     The conference room was a large circus
     audience of white lab coats surrounding
     a theater round seating one large Robot

     Scientists peering through rounded spectacles
     Programs covering their sneering soft whispers
     Is it really winning when no one admires you?

     the typical iron man of the fifties, round head
     A slight green tinge to the metal rivets locking
     arms to torso to legs; a computer chest beeped

The one eyed crocodile was worthwhile, Jimmy shot two rolls of film on him
then ran to meet up with Mr. Kent in the auditorium, So what have you heard?

     Well, Jimmy, it seems this scientist has engineered
     an EM field that generates electrons, perpetually
     The wide open community is talking of nothing else

     He is a relative unknown in and surprisingly enough
     he holds a degree from Sheep's Gates University,

     Where?

     Precisely, Jimmy. No one here knows anything about him
     But one day he writes a paper and has a Robot that works

from this power, constantly regenerating, always charged

        But Mr. Kent, is it alive?

I am not sure, but it just might be. There is certainly occasion
its more than a feeling but less than a dream come true, imagine
if there is really an unending source of power, it would equal
all men – resources available to all – the few would be many

The lights dimmed and the professor took the podium
For many years I have dreamed of a day when all could
walk in the sunlight or swim the warm undisturbed waters

        I have neglected my family for thirty eight years of mediocrity
        This is the bed and pillow on which I have rested and dreamed

        And when I throw this switch it is not I that will light
        up but an EM field from which all things good will flow

        Power from power to light the hearths and homes
        of all peoples from all lands into one world united
        fed, clothed, sheltered. From this we all shall eat

The room dimmed and the Professor looked at the switch
Jimmy Olsen snapped the moment when the lever pulled
Down and the green man's eyes quivered alive with power

        This machine man is not all this small EM Field can operate!
        This small apparatus will power cities, space stations, and cars

        heat homes for miles around

Clark Kent adjusted his eyeglasses at the sight of the Robot
He scribbled away in his notebook, This could help the globe
Research scientist uncorked champagne, and Jimmy shot it all

        Stand! take up thy place and walk
        Immediately the Robot was whole
        generating power on its own

    Then, the Robot shook
    Raised its arms and **Blast!**
    The hands shot a circular force outward

Radiating green forces bursting forth accelerating towards the gathered scientists
washing up and over – then up again the Robot raised his arms over head – **Blast**
Green shot high up reaching out towards the sandbags and the

        ceiling cracked

            plaster falling

                down down down

    And **Blast**

            The Robot jettisons itself up
            flying towards the open sky

I'll call Superman, Jimmy says and pulls the secret knob on his wrist watch
This will signal him to where we are.
I'm only supposed to use this in emergencies

        if this isn't an emergency I don't know what is Jimmy.
        Clark Kent said huddled under their chairs, I'm going
        down there to see if I can help. Jimmy you stay here
        and wait for Superman to arrive and let him know

            But, Mr. Kent, that's not a good idea I think … Clark?
            in a blink   he was gone
                        Jimmy felt suddenly cold

red followed the green streaked sky
        Using his X-Ray vision
        Superman plotted his course

        He could follow the EM field
        as if it was a trail of bread crumbs

He flew back to the auditorium and found Jimmy
He told him that he had met Kent earlier and knew
the situation was unsafe but what was causing this?

        Superman, I am glad to see you!
        Cried the Professor; My Robot

        I … it … flew away

Do you know why?

        No, it was working perfectly in the lab
        Nothing like this should have happened
                My calculations predicted a power surge to eliminate the
excess power it created but it should have been processed into storage containers
        specifically harnessed to recharge the robot and thus produce …

Superman now understood,

        Like a rag doll caught in a gyre
        the robots discharge spun chance

Can it be turned off?

        No
        But … someone must have tampered with it … but who ?

Up
Up
and away

he could think of plenty of people, Lex Luthor for one, or the Nazi's

Superman knew what to do
whatever happened he must stop that robot
from hurting anyone, or worse yet falling into the wrong hands

FOLLOW THE CONTINUING ADVENTURES OF SUPERMAN IN THE NEXT EXCITING EPISODE WHEN SUPERMAN MUST STOP A RENEGADE ROBOT ACTING ON ORDERS FROM SOME UNKNOWN FOE. WE'LL SEE YOU RIGHT HERE IN 30 DAYS TIME SUPERFRIENDS!!! NEVER BELIEVE IT'S NOT SO!

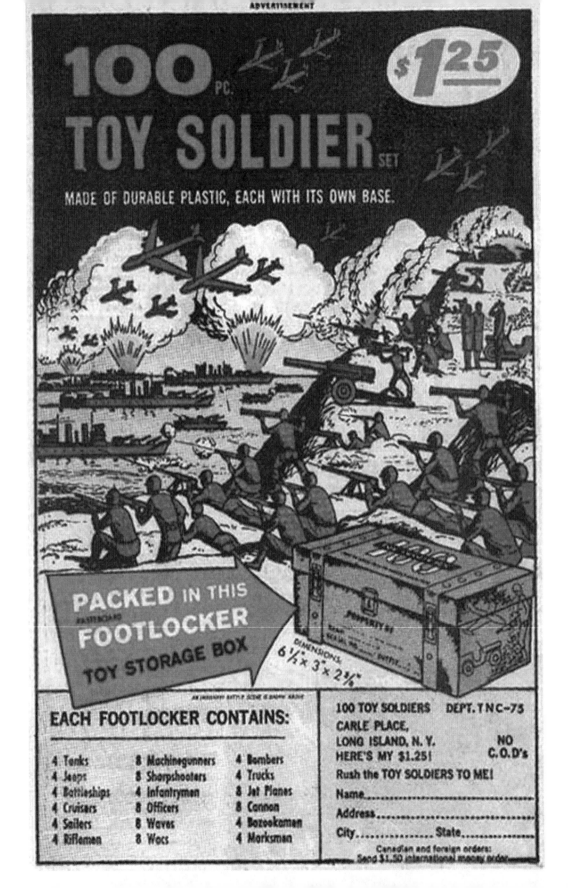

Canto 45

United Nations chartered
Atomic Bomb
Flag raised on Iwo Jima

FDR dies

Harry Truman becomes President
Victory in Europe
Victory in Japan
Japan and Germany surrender

The panel showing the explosion is astonishingly abstract art.

full of astronomical and weather symbols

little planets with rings like Saturn,
star shapes, lightning bolts intertwined,
a figure like an Aurora Borealis.

full of spirals, and other kinds of geometric figures.

During the Silver Age, artists regularly used abstract panels
to convey time travel, passage to a new dimension, and other state changes.

This Golden Age story uses it to describe an explosion that gives birth to a super-hero.
It is a different use of abstract art. The panel is beautiful. It is also full of energy and visual
excitement, as are many of the panels in this tale.

Post
Golden
Age

Canto 46

The Author's Apology for Heroic Poetry and Heroic License

TO THE RIGHT HONOURABLE
HAROLD BLOOM, PROFESSOR EMERITUS OF ARTS AND
LETTERS, YALE UNIVERSITY
LORD CHAMBERLAIN OF HER MAJESTY'S CANON,
KNIGHT OF THE MOST NOBLE ORDER OF THE GARTER, ETC.

My dear Bloom,

It comes within the compass of my power to express all the duty I own, and to pay some duty to our methods of looking upon the world of Literature; so far have your honorable favors outstripped all means to manifest my humble affection that there is nothing left but writing and wondering. There is a sleek serpent that breeds in many minds, feeding only upon forgetfulness and bringing forth, into birth, all but ingratitude and ignorance. To show that I have not been bitten by that monster, for wyrms prove monsters in this age, which yet never any painter could counterfeit to express the ugliness, nor any poet describe to decipher the height of their illness, I have presumed to tender these Madrigals only as remembrances of my service and witnesses of your Lordship's liberal hand, by which I have lived so long, and from your honorable mind that so much have all liberal sciences. In this I shall be most encouraged if your Lordship vouches the protection of my choice of a modern epic brought about upon the occasion of such a loose, low brow character set, for that both your greatness and your judgment in poetry avant garde best may. For without flattery be it spoke, those that know your Lordship know this, that using this science fiction as a recreation, as your Lordship has over gone most of them that make it a practice. Right Honorable Lord, I hope it shall not be distasteful to number you here amongst the favorers of poetry avant garde, and its practitioners, no more than Kings and Emperors that have been desirous to be in the roll of astronomers, that being but a star fair, the other an angel's choir.

The worth of this poem is too well known to need commendation, so I thank you in advance and understand your silent nod. As are the flights of heroic poetry's fancy in a culture bereft of the heroic. The poet knew beforehand the sort of achievement possible the hero required for the present state of affairs, whether capable of writing it or not. Well aware what had been done by previous writers and what is done by contemporaries. This twenty first century has its duty to reverberate within the nature and wit of the poet in that poet's surrounding. All that is fit to print should a printer find.

morality[1]

The silliest way to defend the Western Canon
is to insist it incarnates all of the seven deadly
moral virtues that make up our supposed range
of normative values and democratic principles.

This is palpably untrue...

The West's greatest writers
are subversive of all values,
both ours and their own.

Scholars who urge us to find the source of our morality
and our politics in Plato, or in Isaiah, are out of touch
with the social reality in which we live.

If we read the Western Canon to form
our social, political, or personal moral values,
I firmly believe we will become monsters of selfishness and exploitation.

To read in the service of any ideology is not, in my judgment, to read at all.

You feel strongly; trust to those feelings, it will take its shape and proportions as a tree does from the vital principle that actuates it. I too do not think that great poems can be cast in a morals mould. It sits the same in our dear friend Mr. Coleridge, who contrasts organic form, shaping and developing within, with mechanical regularity not necessarily arising out of the properties of the material, "as when to a mass of wet clay we give whatever shape we wish it to retain when hardened." On this principle of organic form an infinite number of right forms exist: if a poem is shaped and developed from within it will grow like as a creature, living, and the living shape it takes must depend upon how the infection or idea grows and expands in the poet's imagination.

At the top of the hierarchy of former poesies, the pre-fab king, the literary beast tackled, the Heroic Epic is upheld by an immense body of critical theory. Indeed, so important is the Heroic Epic in the Western Canon we have for a millennia derived moral, aesthetic, and religious actions demanding from the world blind desires, driven passions over inner fears, while abandoning ourselves in the bad habits and illogical thinking of self acting heroes. This world has gradually become marvelously variegated, frightful, meaningful, soulful, it has acquired the color of April snow -- but We have been the colorists, acting like the wise cracking

---

[1]

© 1994, The collected poetry of Harold Bloom. *The Western Canon: The Poem as it should be*

cop on the edge: it is the human intellect that has made appearances appear and transported its erroneous basic conceptions into things.

Poetry is meant to effect continuity and transmission of heroic values

on the battlefield the solitary hero dies

I too feel quite alone these days in defending the hero
to a violent warrior culture who needs to be psychoanalyzed
and find a stately later age gentleman to hold

a large-hearted liberality,
or better yet social democracy
is needed to glorify the valor of man

The Society revolves around the strong, and it is the weak that need protecting

The honored
heroic   code

The warrior select is the fundamental of the western canon

between his lord and the sword of an assassin,
the thane of Northumbria is an oft-related example of how

a gift of armor and horses and land is no mere literary convention

a formal battle strategy as organization
to garner a garter within the legends
of Immortality's song of feats ultimate
among excellence, among excess

the heroic ethos contains reality

on the battlefield the solitary hero dies

The poesy of the Reformation is a boil that festers when not curbed by good taste, and when the flow stops the poem very properly stops with it. There were, it has been said, exact patterns of different kinds of poetry laid up in some haven to which the true scholar might arise in his contemplations and show the way towards the true poem. The poet of the eighteenth century sat down to write not a poetry but rather a poem and that poem sat within a certain identity, a form within the recognized form, a poetry which belonged to all but kept rather to itself and did not play well with others. The reader too knew what was fast approaching and feared to tread naught for what ever faerie dance might a flute bring and expecting a goal responded to by rules set forth by the poet's predecessors, who acting upon the good tidings of Horace, or mere wit. What influence these ideal patterns had, what reverence they evoked, is scarcely conceivable now within a time of no mythologies or levitations; nothing to counter the uncontrolled controls and converge upon untouchable prophets and their sons steeping in absolute truth.

I say tell you true, The time is fast approaching, and now is when the dead poem shall hear the voice of the present: and they that hear shall live. He that hears my word, and believeth in him the poets sent before, have an everlasting literature. A literature passing from poem into poetry and poetry towards a Poetry. As we find in John: For as the Father hath life in himself; so hath he given to the Son to have life in himself. But if you believe not this heroic epic, how shall we ever find belief in words?

Precipices and cataracts may be more dramatic per se than a field of toilets but both are American standards full of flashing penetrative insight revealing beauty as the union of the shapely with the vital. It is the subjects chosen for works of art should be such as really are capable of being expressed and conveyed within the limits of those arts. Art is the power of placing a word where none existed before.

on the battlefield the solitary hero dies

The purpose of Anglo-Saxon epic, particularly the Germanic
heroic poetry, the authority pictured obligations, responsibilities,
to glean wisdom in the body politic and not spit in an eye
a useful lessons to garner moral sanctions governing behavior

an abstract reflection of Anglo-Saxon society

a sense of self reflection acting on itself
to out do the hero of the page to rule the Word
a selling back of sorts toward its medium
from which it was first purchased

the group glorifying the bravery of the few
This pragmatic view of heroic poetry is supported

discriminate the monsters to destroys is
to maintain commitment to community
heroism is maintaining civilization

venturing towards battles against evil
the constant vigilance is constant vengeance
is this not the way of Pax Americana

But precisely this: we seek out the hero, and let us not be ungrateful to such resolute fellows who have played the role for our poets to transcribe perspectives and valuations of their spirit, with apparent mischievousness and futility. To see differently in this century, to *want* to see differently, is no small discipline and preparation for a future objectivity. Henceforth, my dear Professor Bloom, let us be on guard against the dangerous old conceptual fiction that posited a pure, painless, timeless knowing subject; let us guard against the snares of contradictory concepts as pure reason, absolute spirituality, knowledge in itself; as these always demand of an eye of absurdity and nonsense.

the aesthetic[2]

its best defense is the experience of reading King Lear
King Lear does not derive from a crisis in philosophy,
nor can its power be explained away as a mystification
somehow promoted by the bourgeois institutions.

It is a mark of the degeneracy of literary study
that one is considered an eccentric for holding
that the literary is not dependent upon the philosophical,

and that the aesthetic is irreducible to ideology
or worse to mere metaphysics. Aesthetic criticism
returns us to the autonomy of imaginative literature

the sovereignty of the solitary soul, the reader not
        as a person in society

        but as the deep self,
        our ultimate inwardness.

Thus most humbly submitting myself and my labors and whatever is or may be in me to your Lordship's protection, I humbly end, wishing your Lordship as continual an increasing of health and honor as there is a daily increase of virtue to come to happiness.

2

© 1994, The collected poetry of Harold Bloom. *The Western Canon: The Poem sublime*

Canto 47

Marshall Plan
Jackie Robinson plays for the Dodgers

movies purged of communists
television spreads

first around the world commercial airline service
first supersonic aircraft

Joe Louis beats "Jersey Joe"
Walcott

Legion of Superheroes
The Hall of Justice

Superman is morally troubled with the kind of authority figure he has become.

Calling a joint meeting of all superheroes in the known universe
        sponsored by the Justice League of America inviting all
        Renegades and groups alike to hear the Superman's talk

The House of Thunder collides

Captain Marvel and Mary Marvel, Nightwing sits in the shadow of Batman. The
House of Lanterns, as agents of an alien power meld, Captain Atom, Blue Beetle,
Wonder Girl, Flash, Slipstream, Captain Comet, and the female Dr. Light, Rip
Hunter, Jonah Hex, Tommy Tomorrow, Space Ranger, and possibly even Barry
Allen, Jason Blood, the Spectre, Zatara, Dr. Fate, and Deadman, Raven, Cyborg,
Hawk, and Changeling, Starfire gather around in a circle.

Hawkman sits by Wonder Woman who is having coffee with the Flash, Batman
broods in a corner as Robin engages Aquaman on air and sea; They are all here,
even the Green Lantern who is trading tricks with the Green Arrow, even those
once thought dead have gathered within these hall under an immunity of sort, all as
247 brothers and sisters in garb coming together wondering what this is all for.

I have asked you all here today to use your powers against something your powers are not
designed to be used against. We fight villains and villainy requires different methods to
subdue than other troubling developments in the world. It is one thing to smash a brick wall
and another to save one life, or a group of lives. To save a life often times means to smash a
brick wall as our missions deem fit, and smashing is what we are good at doing. The way we
escape and capture is what makes us great. But today, there is exists a greater problem,
one which prisons will not contain. The Joker can plan to destroy a city but he cannot create
or dismiss hunger. We all have felt it, metaphorically and physically, seen it, and often reject
this from our daily lives to continue the struggle against evil. It is all consuming, however

Hunger Ravages

In Eritrea, Uganda, Djibouti, and Kenya
Somalia, The Sudan and Further south

Hunger Ravages the peoples of this world

Please remember the millions of people throughout Africa
who continue to suffer from famine caused by war and drought.
We have received urgent requests for famine relief from Angola,
the Democratic Republic of Congo, and Namibia.

The number of children in the drought-hit
Kiptangwany area, Nakuru District,
has dropped by about 50 percent

A nine-year-old in the Muriricua Province,
said his parents could only afford to provide supper,
a small lump of ugaii taken with plain water.

Hunger Ravages the peoples of this world
People can barely concentrate due to hunger
This the most serious food shortage in a decade.

people chew pieces of waffa for lunch

Mr Ekeno Ewoi died after eating keiapple fruits.
He collapsed on the road near his home as he was
going to search for more keiapples at a fence nearby

A massive aid operation is unfolding across drought stricken parts of Ethiopia. But pockets of famine in the south and southeast demonstrate the continued need for special attention in some parts of the country.

There is also instability in the south-east, frequent reports of banditry and rebel incursions from Somalia and Sudan. Some international aid agencies have pulled their workers out because of the danger.

Hunger Ravages

In Eritrea, Uganda, Djibouti, and Kenya
Somalia, The Sudan and Further south
Hunger Ravages

In the north nearly 2.7 million people face severe food shortages,
making it the second most severely hit country after Ethiopia.
But, you say there is always such shortages of food that this sounds usual, or normal

Relief efforts have been hindered by looting and fighting,
which led to the temporary suspension of food distribution
These countries have a reputation as a difficult and dangerous
place for aid workers.

Crop failure and fighting between rival militias left 1.5 million people at risk
Harvests are expected to fail for the sixth year
there have been outbreaks of cholera
child malnutrition estimates in the millions

Hunger Ravages

In Eritrea, Uganda, Djibouti, and Kenya
Somalia, The Sudan and Further south
Hunger Ravages

Many families survive on one meal a day, depending on cactus fruits, wild berries and leaves
for food.
the food crisis could spread
people are threatened by food shortages

Thousands of farmers in the grain-producing regions
in the south have fled from the conflict zones,
leaving crops wanting, waiting for harvest

water holes have reached dangerously low levels, and livestock are dying
Many people a   re already leaving rural areas for the cities, in search of
more food and water

As a result there have been sharp rises in local food prices
and livestock herds are being sold at fallen prices

The border war has also burdened the country

Hunger Ravages

In Eritrea, Uganda, Djibouti, and Kenya
Somalia, The Sudan and Further south

Where shall we buy bread to feed all these people?
Let us turn a phrase: Bread like poetry is for everyone
Gather together the leftovers, so nothing will be wasted

Canto 48

Berlin airlift
        Truman reelected
Alger Hiss indicted

Polaroid camera introduced
        term "cold war' coined
vitamin B-12 cures pernicious
anemia

There is no life on Bizarro World

Brought into being by the ingenious duplicator ray
        built by Lex Luthor, the renegade scientist
        Superman's bitterest enemy, Bizarro is lifeless
matter in human form - a thing composed of unloving matter

The first Bizarro, it is said, was an inadequate clone of Superboy
        envisioned by a scientist in Smallville
        How bizarre! he said at meeting his double
the dim creature heard and adopted Bizarro as its name.

In a covert mission Lex Luthor stole the plans from the Smallville scientist
        creating his own duplicator ray powered by an EM field
        He was able to reconstruct the apparatus and create his own
Bizarro - a grotesque imitation of the adult Superman: A Thing of Steel.

        a blundering menace,

His black hair is scruffy and tousled.
He is well-meaning but witless, and dim
His speech is illiterate and ungrammatical

Me not human... me not creature, moans Bizarro ... me not even animal!

a misshapen, imperfect duplicate of Superman,
Clad in an invulnerable masquerade of Superman
and endowed with all of his mighty super powers

He reveals a sad pathetic, grotesque creature

His flesh is chalk white, and his face appears plated
as though chiseled out of rock.

an artificial imitation that came out unsatisfactory!
owning only a dim copy of Superman's keen mind

Bizarro rules the far-distant planet Htrae, a mixed up, crazy world
all men are imperfect imitations of Superman
all women are distorted doubles of Lois Lane

It is to distinguish himself from all these other male Bizarros
that the original Bizarro wears a large medallion around his neck
identifying himself as Bizarro No. 1

Indeed, although the name Bizarro is used as a proper noun, designating Bizarro himself, it
is also employed in the texts as a general term to designate any Bizarro creature.

All Bizarros are imperfect duplicates of other living things;
artificial imitations that came out imperfect!
the most famous monsters of all time
Crafted by the evil Lex Luthor

The Secret Laboratory of Lex Luthor

The panel is quite beautiful.
It is also full of visual energy and excitement,

This was a Golden Age super-hero constructed of Lead
Lex Luthor prepares a boiling chemical cauldron

All of the lab scenes are impressively drawn.
They are full of boiling chemicals,
and billowing clouds of smoke.
Most of the clouds are carefully composed
to create interesting geometric patterns.

Much of this story celebrates Luthor's masculinity
typical male desire to be strong, as beauty to female

and the way the hero's body becomes literally made

He celebrates this. Also, he now can interface with the forces of physics, such as magnetism and electricity, and machines that use these forces.

This too plays on a male fascination with machines.

The story allows men to fantasize about their bodies
being linked to worlds of machinery.
This is a very gratifying set of ideals.
The ideas are developed into an almost poetic grandeur here.

Both the story concepts, and their depiction in Bizarro, are memorably intense.

In fancy blue uniform,
In clearly idealized figures
It is a brilliant red
It continues the metal theme

A computer made of steel, full of punch cards & rivets,
like one might apply to a girder at the construction site.

Luthor is dressed in a white lab coat working on his experiments.
This white outlook and spotless white uniforms create direct, open
associations of the modernity in this era. the Scientific will prevail

in momentous enterprises of advancement

Luthor is something of a solitary character throughout this first story.
The tale mainly concentrates on Bizarro himself, and the wonders of this new body.

It depicts many landscapes,
relating to many kinds of machinery,
from the science lab
to the motorcycle at the end.

Me unhappy! Bizarro affirms sadly,
Me don't belong in world of living people!
Me don't know difference between right and wrong - good and evil!

And that my friend is what makes you special,
says Luthor, as well as my creation and friend.

Did you know that in the Chinese Language the symbol representing people
is two marks, one large stroke going upwards the other smaller supporting

Do you know which part you are Bizarro? He didn't wait for an answer …

You my dim friend are the smaller supporting stroke. For without small support
of the strong the larger mark will fall down and then the whole will never stand

Me stand in the way of all things ….

He was interrupted by the radio announcing
The fight against famine waged by Superman
The Justice League and the caped crusaders
organizing the largest single global effort
to eradicate hunger, the staging of food
will take place at Pier 623 …   beerrrst

Lex Luthor threw a wingtip shoe towards
the radio breaks in a solid white hummm

In the distance begins an ending that will never have a core
No not this time my grotesque replica. You are going to be
Superman, well not a super superman but superman enough

This is the eve of annihilation for that boob the people all hail
heralding high above, hailing him as the savior of the brute
a common man finds strength in his short sighted deeds

But with you and I operating against him, we shall turn tides
and let the people see his true side. In an age old deception
You will bungle this so called fight against famine and waste
all the donations into the seas. The bread will sink into the seas

       Me think bread walk on water, Mr. Luthor
       Me see crusts float, but then get soggy then

Yes, and then my fine fellow, what did the crust do then?
Did it sink then after wallowing in its doom, like the fly
struggling in the web only tangling itself further frustrated
by blind desires of freedom looming off in the distance
only to have it smacked out of hand by its predictor? Well!?!

       Me see the wet crust eat up by a brown bizarro duck.

Confusion not curiosity killed the cat my friend, but in this case
you are making me more mad than a rained on rooster. Do you
understand the plan as you are to perform it? This is important

       Me unhappy! Bizarro affirms again, but me do.
       Me don't belong in world of living people!
       Living people will know soon I am not Superman

Not if you keep to the plan. Stay away from cameras and as you say Living people.

Pier 623

       The large cargo ship tied to the dock of the pier
       stretched as far as the eye could pay tribute
       to advancements over the maritime and water

       Support came in my the millions. Bruce Wayne
       Donated all of the resources of Wayne industries

       The angles of the earth people poured out for the poor
       The Flash raced around the world in return for donations

       The Green Arrow was more direct, making throats quiver

       Wonder Woman gathered aid from the Amazon tribes
       Jonah Hex raided hell, while Aquaman raised the oceans

       Tommy Tomorrow and Space Ranger still have not returned
       but have radioed ahead of their success from Alpha Centari

       Lois Lane was on hand to report of the final loading

She pictured with Bruce Wayne, So Bruce why all this?

>   I am not a leader of man but a captain of business
>   and business must return to the earth what it takes
>   And Superman makes one heck of an impression

Is Superman the only reason outside of a huge tax break

>   why Ms. Lane you take me for a cynic

No I'm just paid to ask the tough questions.
By the way where is the man of the hour?

>   I think he's off to the mountains
>   afraid they might make him king
>   Let's continue this over dinner …

But then the sun looked suddenly small in the grown light

The panel showing the explosion is astonishingly abstract art

>   full of astronomical and weather symbols

>   >   little planets with rings like Saturn,
>   >   star shapes, lightning bolts intertwined,
>   >   a figure like an Aurora Borealis.

>   full of spirals, and other kinds of geometric figures.

During the Silver Age, artists regularly used abstract panels
to convey time travel, passage to a new dimension, and other state changes.

This Golden Age story uses it to describe an explosion that gives birth to a super-hero.
It is a different use of abstract art. The panel is beautiful. It is also full of energy and visual
excitement, as are many of the panels in this tale.

>   Bruce Wayne and Lois Lane looked out towards the exploding ship
>   the hope and survival of millions of people discharged as heat light

>   workers in Yellow hard hats ran circling patterns to escape
>   the flames of the burning bags of grains, scent of crumpets

>   The toaster clicking, jumping into the fire jumping far away
>   The sirens set the pieces in place, they once fit if they could
>   put it together, but the flames rose higher, and up up away

>   >   was the famous red cape
>   >   the streak unmistakable

>   It was Superman rising

>   Communication to base
>   we have visuals on target

>   The red and blue summersault
>   fanned flames, Lois Lane cried
>   While Superman seemed to cry

tears of joy
streamed down
the chalk white
beveled cheeks

this was of course
bizarre
I know the pieces fit!

in seconds the Batman, the dark knight of Gotham City was on hand

But it was over before it could begin
Superman from no where destroyed
all that he built in one swoop

Batman
Aquaman
Green Lantern
and Lois Lane

loomed betrayal
How this?

It was hours before the fire subsided
To the west the Green Lantern pointed

Flying low over the sea the man of steel

approaching he called,
It is I, do not be afraid

I am aware from the reports you believe that I am responsible for this
This is a pure detective story
there are no elements of fantasy or science fiction that cannot explain

This is an archetypal tale about a phony medium.
Comic books regularly ran such stories, right up

a full range of fake "supernatural" events
we need to warn the public about this con

I tell you truly, you are looking for me not because you saw signs,
but because you saw from your eyes and not from your heart

Do not work for the food that perishes,
but rather for the food that lasts forever,

But it was the policeman's handcuff's that welcomed him home

Officer Smicknicolic asked politely, if you will Superman,
Please respect the order of the law. You are under arrest
and even though you can bend steel bars I will ask again
that you do nothing to hamper this action of justice

Superman lifted his drooping arms

        the shame from saving
            all the times the planet

for the humanitarian service a mistake clicked silver handcuffs
      this was all symbolic but when his head slammed the door
      as he was ushered into the police's backseat he knew fake

        or not there was real hatred for him
        if rocks could injure they would fly

      In another scene
      Lex Luthor clasped joy
      in his hands wrung serenity

       and the world gasps

Canto 49

NATO formed

final 16 civil war veterans hold
last meeting
American Communist leaders
convicted

UN headquarters dedicated
Yankees beat the Dodgers

cortisone discovered
Joe Louis retires

All things being equal the simplest explanation is the correct one
as it is in every episode of Matlock, the one accused is not guilty
    She primps her bind fold and tips her scales
    are you telling me we should take this all on

    faith

The Daily Planet reported the loss of the ship, 108 lives,
unprecedented world wide unity to shelter and feed all

    humans

    in all countries

    bread would mean life

    still, the hungry were left to their hunger

in the moments of the night I can count the dead
if ever we were partners you and I you must know
that the struggle is only for itself, nothing more

    the only thing we find is that we only have one another

Conservative voices called for tougher restrictions on superhero movements
    Liberal mothers called into question his further role as a model
    Congress commissioned a grand inquiry, but all mouths wilted

One thing was sure, there was going to be a trial, super strength or not he would stand tall
before a real human and explain himself. He will be held responsible and accountable. The
hell you say, he'll be sentenced to death, or worse the Phantom Zone. If this was possible at
all, for what does one do with an errant Superman? Do you place him in exile and hope he
never returns? How do you kill one who has saved so much?

    How do you solve a problem like Superman

Well I for one believe him, Bruce Wayne told Lois over dinner

The cuisine of Thailand is as exotic as it is subtle,
fresh, timeless, traditional and well tested, the food
of the ancient Kingdom blends exquisite alchemy

and surprise.

I don't know what he was thinking but I will always love him,
Lois said into her onion soup, what do you think will happen,
Where is he being held? Is there an investigation? What is …

Finally, the dinner bell announces the time has come to indulge in culinary delight in the
congenial atmosphere of the informal dining room's eclectic decor.

He has voluntarily restricted himself to his quarters
in the Hall of Justice awaiting a trial of some sorts, but who
would try him? What court falls into jurisdiction? For him or
any super hero, for that matter, who is free of form or vision
to offer an opinion on this matter?

magnificent feast of lamb, trout, homemade breads
caramel crème with coconut toastings and mango

developing a reputation of its own among restaurateurs

With a fork in her hand she asks, Who will represent him?

to rival the finest restaurants in the largest cities
creating a vibrant mix of fresh tastes and interesting menus

marinated beef, chicken, ribs, or fresh seafood sizzling
on grills while rosemary aromas waft towards heaven

Pre
Silver
Age

Canto 50

McCarthy seeks Communists
Alger Hiss convicted

Hydrogen Bomb development authorized
color television licensed

Douglas MacArthur Commander of UN
forces in Korea
Jackson Pollack action abstract
expressionism

average weekly earnings reach $60
minimum wage set at $.75/hr

[[[[[[[[[[[[[[[[[[[[[[[[[[[[[[[[[[[Drum Roll]]]]]]]]]]]]]]]]]]]]]]]]]]]]]]]]]]]]
::::: ! ::::: << Cymbal clash <<<<<<<<<<

Now

Faster than a speeding bullet

ssssuuuuuwwwwwsssssssssssssshhhhhhhh

More powerful than a Locomotive

baaaaawwwwhhhhhhooooooooooaaaahhhh woooohaaaahhhhhhh hhhhaaa hhhhhaa

Able to leap tall buildings in a single bound

ssssuuuuuwwwwwssssssssssssssshhhhhhhh

ssssuuuuuwwwwwssssssssssssssshhhhhhhh

It's a bird

No it's a Plane

It's

It's

It's

S u p e r rrr r m a n

That's right Superfan's it's that time again for the Superman Radio Hour, brought to you today by Camel, more doctor's prefer the flavor of Camel any other brand.

[BREAK]

Jimmy Olsen : Gee Mr. White I thought you always smoked a Cigar

Perry White : Not any more Jimmy [sound of tussling hair] Not since I tried a Camel.

Jimmy Olsen : Are they really that good Mr. White?

Perry White : Nothing quite like it. I'd say they were super

[Perry White & Jimmy Olsen : laughing   Fade to theme]

When we last left our Hero he was waiting to stand trial for a crime that he did not commit. But no! The cargo ship of humanitarian aid, sunk to the depths of the seas was committed by the evil Lex Luthor and the bizarre Superman look alike Bizarro! Not one person saw for themselves what had truly happened. And our hero, Superman stood accused. The question of where to try him plagued the people's mind's. Very few stood by Superman's side in these dark times. The Batman, Lois Lane, and Jimmy Olsen and the editor of the Dailey planet, Perry White all remained dedicated to finding out what really had happened. They saw what looked like him attack the ship, but how this? For it was Superman's plan to begin this work in the first place why would he put it asunder?

But none knew of Bizarro's existence, let alone that the evil scientist possessed such a technology. No one could imagine this, but Superman. Superman knew he did not do this. He had flown to his Fortress of Solitude. There was a hullabaloo that needed to be avoided.

But before he could redeem himself the crowd had began to jeer him. Jeer Superman you ask? Yes, The opinion against the heroic Man of Steel was devastating. They had placed faith in him and then, as if to mock their efforts he destroyed it all. It had to be Superman, for who else flies in blue tights and flouts a red cape? What kind of Communist plot was this? What is that S on his chest? Is this Super or is it Soviet, or worse is it Stalin? Is it really and Alien sickle? If so where is his damn commie hammer? He does strike like those propaganda posters we see of mother russia's sons. Is he really an American?

Can we really trust Superman?

And the people began to forget the wondrous deeds. Close the open skies of freedom he has preserved for so many years. The forces that wage against Earth were now up for debate. What would the children think if this Superman was a pinko commie bastard? He could be you know. They are tricky them pinko bastards, they are.

And so an order came down from Capital Hill, and order to effectively place Superman before the House Un-American Activities Committee. Today's Committee's chairman is J. Parnell Thomas, and Robert Stripling, Chief Investigator.

The Chairman: Raise your right hand, please, Superman. Do you solemnly swear the testimony you are about to give is the truth, the whole truth, and nothing but the truth, so help you God?

Superman: I do.

The Chairman: Sit down.

Mr. Stripling: Superman, will you state your name, please, for the record?

Superman: Superman, or Kel-el

Mr. Stripling: That is S-u-p-e-r-m-a-n

Superman: That is right.

Mr. Stripling: Is that your pen name?

Superman: Yes.

Mr. Stripling: Where were you born, Superman?

Superman: On the Planet, Krypton

Mr. Stripling: When did you leave Krypton?

Superman: In the year you would call 1926.

Mr. Stripling: How long have you been on the Earth?

Superman: I have been on the Earth, on and off again, since late 1929, but specifically as a superhero since late 1930's.

Mr. Stripling: Have you been a Superhero anywhere other than the Earth?

Superman: One second. May I have one moment to get this in order?

Mr. Stripling: Yes.

Superman: No, I have never acted as a Superhero on any other planet before the Earth. It is the special light of the yellow sun that enables me to have these powers.

Mr. Stripling: And this is why you are heralded as a hero?

Superman: Yes, thanks to the American public. And No, it is the deeds that I do not the powers I possess that make one a hero.

Mr. Stripling: Now, Superman, you have heard the testimony of Mr. [Lex] Luthor?

Superman: Yes.

Mr. Stripling: You have read the letter I read from Trilling Stanford?

Superman: Yes.

Mr. Stripling: And I am sure you know why you have been brought here and the political implications of what these proceedings are about?

Superman: Yes.

Mr. Stripling: Are you now or have you ever been a member of the communist party?

[[[[[[[[[[[[[[[[[[[[[[[[[[[[[[[[Drum Roll]]]]]]]]]]]]]]]]]]]]]]]]]]]]]]]]

:::::: **!!** :::::: << Cymbal clash <<<<<<<<<<

Canto 51

China and US spar in Korea
UNIVAC computer unveiled

first color TV broadcast
first transcontinental direct-dial telephone
service

first Atomic power produced
New York vs. New York in World Series

Chambers of the House Un-American Activities Committee

In a time when uncertainty appears to be actuality
        Abandoned on a bench

            A small white room sitting in blue chairs
            a circle of white men gathered do decide

        Heroics

            What do we?

weak kneed meek, lost for words
in arm folded rants & lamenting

            Let us also go
            then, that we
            may die with him!

            Thus alone a council then gathered
      It's raining in the arcade outside

            for this man has done what many consider
        in the unforeseen events that have
        drenched, brought to these familiar grounds

            a flag which flies over this mundane park
Moving through, the evil that goes along that flight, that
        takes

the spirited seat he sat unto the end.
a lifeless mirror, on its side.

            Nixon asks Is he even a man?

            A slab

all men believe on him;
the people shall come and take away

both our place and nation.

And one of them said "You know nothing at all,
or even consider that it is expedient for us,

that one man should die for the people,
and that the nation will never perish.

presently   alone

a past or future flawed.

::::: ! ::::: << Cymbal clash <<<<<<<<<<<<

Canto 52

Eisenhower President
inflation up
steel mills seized by Presidential order to end strike

George Meany elected president of the AFL
Walter Reuther made president of the CIO

UFOs sighted everywhere

::::: ! ::::: << Cymbal clash <<<<<<<<<<

Bed Chambers of Bizarro

Me am not me
he is me as I is him

> Actually I am glad you asked this.
> I have been having troubles with my poems late at night.
> They gather in the corners and conspired against me.
> Their I's just glaring at me.
> I know they are up to something but to what
> that is what I don't know.

in him is no the me that isn't me
I can only be pretty me in the deep sky

> bizarro #1
> is there is
> me is em
>
> em eb eh t'nac em
> nac eh em
>
> mih evol em
>
> mih etah em sa
> em etah em sa

To break boat and sink supplies
me save the planet by saving these people

> Me do this for Bizarro-Lois
> as much as anything else
> her will know this is for her
> as he will know this is for him
> we are not the same him and me

112

Maybe a union forming? Maybe a murderous horde? I don't know;
they are all born from me so what they are doing is nefarious
if anything at all.
They are huddled there now.
Like the Collected Works of Olsen
sitting waiting to become something out of their own.
They must be put down.
Put down fast and hard.

      we are not so the same color
      as text floats across the streak blue
      so cloud smear red skies at night
      sailors run in fright from the winter
      snows be carefree the true color will

            saturate the shine and won't let go

      there are some who will not see me for this
      day or night me will know and crunch
      the bow will break the Fincastle white foam

A surgical strike to pull out the evil poems from the good well behaved poems. Look at them over there
that ugly gang of slack jawed verse.
Seething at me? with me as the me that is the me when I am creating
I created you damn it now do what you are told!
Cut the lawn! I'll put you over my knee.

      How tough will you be then?

      Me do this for Bizarro-Lois
      as much as anything else
      her will know this is for her
      and me will be nobody

'cause you're nobody 'til somebody loves you

Canto 53

Korean Armistice
Yankees beat the Dodgers again

Wayne Morse sets record for filibustering
Stereophonic and 3D movies

Rosenbergs executed
Social Security Act broadened

When the Stars sought him at the gorge, they said, Where is he?

Could he have left?

there was murmuring among the people concerning him:

for some said,
He is a good man; protector, friend

others said,
No; he deceives the American child

For there is no man that does anything in secret,
and he himself seeks to be known openly.
If thou do these things, show thyself to the world.

My time is not yet come
but your time is always ready.

The world cannot hate you; but me it hates openly
My power is not mine, If any man will do his will,
he shall know of the city, and metropolis is my home

and from the far corner of the angry crowd emerged a child
shoving an elbow outwards to make his way to stand before

Superman looked at this boy
for a moment a tear

whether it be of America, or whether I speak of myself.

After this Superman walked into the proceedings; alone.

Canto 54

Early Warning RADAR net
CinemaScope
          McCarthy condemned
Five congressmen shot on the floor of the house

first atomic sub commissioned
               Brown vs. Board of Education ruled
against segregation
Hemingway gets Nobel prize for literature

French withdraw from Vietnam
polio vaccine introduced by Jonas Salk

Truth, Justice and The American Way

I am.
the speeding bullet of the world:
capturing dreamlights of being.

see with eyes unclouded

Judge not according to the appearance of presented facts
          but judge rather righteous judgment

You all know me, and You know what it is that

I am

and I have not come for myself, but rather I come for you.
For you to have something of truth to hold onto

I am the speeding bullet of the world:
he that follows me shall not walk in darkness,
but shall capture the dream lights of being.

I will do what I can for the little while am I with you, and then I will go back to him that
created me as do we all go back to the fires that forged our spirit and you shall not find me:

and where I am, thither you cannot come.
Is this not what we came here to seek?

Then said the Stars among themselves,
Where will he go, that we shall not find him?

will he go to another world? fight against us?
A hero who becomes the enemy of his brother.

What manner of saying is this that he said,
Many of the people therefore, when they heard

there was a division among the Stars

You, certainly have verification of yourself;
I feel you & your testimony are not true.

What evidence do you have to support this
You cannot expect us to just go on "take my word on this"

Superman answered and said unto them,

If any man thirst, let him come unto america, and drink.
out of its belly shall flow rivers of living water.

Then said they unto him, Where is your America?

Superman answered, You neither know me, nor my America:
if you had known me, you should have known my America also.

I go my way, and you shall seek me,
and shall die in your filth; where I go, you cannot come.

Then said the Stars, Will he kill himself? what is he saying?

You are from beneath; I am from above
you are of this world; I am not of this world.

Therefore I say to you, you shall die in your crimes

if you believe not I what I say,

your crimes shall die in you

Then said they unto him, Who do you think you are talking to Superman?
The senator rose and pointed a finger at the man of steel

Superman rose too. Stood accused. His eyes aglow.
Open, down the bend barrel of a closed finger.

Here Superman was at his most gallant.
Never once showed malice, nor distain

however they understood that he stood against them
that he stood for the America he has always fought for

And Superman spoke to them,

I do nothing of myself; but as America has taught me, I act when I am needed to act.

I have many things to say and to judge of you but I speak to the world
to those who have suffered because of another's action in my namesake.

These things which I have heard of him, upset me as it does you.
It is distressing that these proceedings hamper efforts that save life.
Once this situation is settled we shall make all things right again.

America has not left me alone;
I do always those things that please

As he spoke these words, his approval rating soared

Then said Superman to those Stars which believed on him,
If you continue in my word, then are you my heroes indeed;

And you shall know the truth, and the truth shall make you free.

His answer was anger, This committee
has never been in bondage to any man.

How dare you Superman!
You shall be made free? Ha.

I say to you, Whosoever commits crime is the servant of crime .
If the poetry shall make you free, you shall be free indeed.
I know that you are America's seed; but you seek to kill me,
because my word has no place in you.

I speak of things which I have seen in my America
and you do that which you have seen in your America.

They answered and said unto him, America is our America.

Superman smiled his super smile,
If you were America's children,
you would do the works of America.
But now you seek to kill me,
a man that has told you the truth,

I have heard of America: this did not America.

Then said they to him,
We are not born of multiples;
we have one America, balanced America, America the beautiful.

there is no rational truth in you Superman.
your America the devil the lusts a murderer from the beginning

for you are a coward of strength,
and the America you shield
yourself behind.

We can smell the borscht that bleached that red cape of yours.

When he speaks his words are of fear, not a lie, but of a semper fear
he speaks of his own fear, the fear of his family, his home and land

He that is of America hears America's words: you therefore hear them not,

because the Stars believe you not.
because you are not of America.

because we tell you the truth,
because you believe us not.

[There was a long hush over the crowded trees in the forest that night]

Superman answered, I am not a devil; I honor my America, and you dishonor me.
And I seek not mine own glory:
there is one that seeks and another who judges and another to keep

Superman said unto them,
before Washington was,

I am

Canto 55

First filmed Presidential press conference
Geneva Conference
SEATO Treaty signed
Rosa Park's bus boycott
AFL/CIO merger
racial segregation in schools banned by
Supreme Court
Davy Crockett fad
Rock & Roll
Dodgers beat the Yankees

From: US Congress. Senate.
Committee on the Judiciary. Juvenile Delinquency.
Report presented to Senate 1955
1955-6. Library of Congress Catalogue Card Number 77-90720

84th Congress
1st Session SENATE Report
No. 62

Comic Books and Juvenile Delinquency

Interim Report of the Committee on the judiciary
pursuant to S. Res. 89 and S. Res. 190
(83d Cong. 1st Sess.) - (83d Cong. 2d Sess.)
A Part of the Investigation of Juvenile Delinquency in the United States

Committee on the Judiciary
Harley M. Kilgore, West Virginia, Chairman

... When looking at the question: What are "comic books?" we find that many, including all those with which the subcommittee's investigation was concerned, were found to be neither humorous nor books. They are thin, 32-page pamphlets usually trimmed to 7 by 10 1/2 inches. Most of them sell for 10 cents a copy. They are issued monthly, bimonthly, quarterly, semiannually, or as one-time publications. They are wire-stitched in a glossy paper cover on which, in the crime and horror type, there has been printed in gaudy colors an often grim and lurid scene contrived to intrigue prospective purchasers into buying them. The inside page contain from 3 to 5 stories told in pictures with balloon captions. The pictures are artists' line drawings printed in color, intended to tell part of the story by showing the characters in action. In the case of crime and horror comic books, the story and the action are often quite horrendous.

... The pattern for present-day comic books was set in 1935 when New Fun, a 64-page collection of original material printed in four colors, was put on the newsstands. Action Comics were put on sale in 1938, and Superman Quarterly Magazine appeared in 1939. The number of comic book publishers has increased and the circulation figures have risen astonishingly since that time.

... It has been estimated conservatively that in 1940 publishers of at least 150 comic-book titles had annual revenues of over 20 million. Ten years later, in 1950 about 300 comic-book titles were being published with annual revenues of nearly 41 million. The upswing in the next 3 years brought the number of titles to over 650 and the gross to about 90 million.3 Average monthly circulation jumped from close to 17 million copies in 1940 to 68 million in 1953.

... In the years between 1945 and 1954, two striking changes took place in the comic-book industry. The first was the great increase in the number of comic books published and the number of firms engaged in their publication. The second was the increase numbers of comic books dealing with crime and horror and featuring sexually suggestive and sadistic illustrations. This increase of materials featuring brutality and violence is being offered to any child who has the 10-cent purchase price. That these examples of crime and horror are aimed at children is clearly evident from the advertisements with which each issue is replete.

... A view of the steps involved in producing and distributing a comic book affords some insight into the problems confronting the industry in determining an editorial content acceptable for reading by children. While ultimate responsibility for editorial content rests with the publishers, their training and backgroups vary widely. One, for example, combines publication of comic books with an active law practice. Some publish "girlie" magazines and comic books from the same editorial office. Some publish well-known pocket-sized book editions. One man publishes both comic books and the pseudomedical type of sex books. Several include pseudoscience books among their publications. One fact is clearly noted: A background in knowledge of child education and development is not a requisite to becoming a publisher of crime and horror comic books designed for children.

... The widely diverse assortment of publications, which might be routed by distributor to the wholesaler and in turn to the retail newsdealer, was shown in the prepared exhibits of some of the magazines distributed by the Kable News Co. These exhibits, which were introduced at the New York hearings, included such titles as: Suppressed, The Facts About Modern Bootlegging, Mysteries, Billy Bunny, Exhibit Homes, Haunted Thrills, Zip, Romance Time, Nifty, Homecraft, Mystery Tales of Horror and Suspense, Picture Scope, Magazine Digest, Masked Ranger, Gala, Danger, Voodoo, The Children's Hour, Wham, Radio-Electronics, Pack O' Fun, Strange Fantasy, Exclusive, Dare, Frolic, Child Life, Fantastic Fears, Universe, Tops, He, Hunting and Fishing, Danger, and Tab. The covers of many of these publications carried pictures of scantily clad females in suggestive poses. The titles of some of the article as featured on the covers were: "The Lady Is a Man," "All-Year Vacation Home," "Sex Before Marriage," "I Was Forced Into Russia's Fifth Column," "I Sold Myself in the Marriage Racket," "Athletes Are Lousy Sports," "What's New in Transistors," "Babes in Boyland," "The Prodigal Son," "Backstage at Burlesk," "The Smart Drummer," "Rica Rita- Pantie Model," "Angel of the Battlefields," "Sexie Tessie Up North," "Joseph and His Brothers," "Tommy's Bedroom Secret," "Dead End Kids of Space," "Are Bosomy Beauties a Fad?" "Are Vets Freeloading Medical Care?" "Sixty Lady-Killers on the Loose," "Evelyn West vs. Kinsey," "Are Our Churches Really Red?" "The Beauty Is a Witch," "Slaves to Beauty," "Trouble in Morocco," "Court of Immoral Women," "Backlashes? Try Educating Your Thumb," and "Where Bad Girls Make Good."

The Nature of Crime and Horror Comic Books

... It has been pointed out that the so-called crime and horror comic books of concern to the subcommittee offer short courses in murder, mayhem, robbery, rape, cannibalism, carnage, necrophilia, sex, sadism, masochism, and virtually every other form of crime, degeneracy, bestiality, and horror. These depraved acts are presented and explained in illustrated detail in an array of comic books being bought and read daily by thousands of children. These books evidence a common penchant for violent death in every form imaginable. Many of the books dwell in detail on various forms on insanity and stress sadistic degeneracy. Others are devoted to cannibalism with monsters in human form feasting on human bodies, usually the bodies of scantily clad women.

SPECIFIC EXAMPLES OF MATERIAL DEALT WITH AT NEW YORK HEARING

To point out more specifically the type of material being dealt with, a few typical examples of story content and pictures were presented at the New York hearings on April 21, 1954. From the few following examples, it will be clearly seen that the major emphasis of the material then available on America's newsstands from this segment of the comic book industry dealt with depraved violence:

Story No. 1

Bottoms Up (Story Comics)

This story has to do with a confirmed alcoholic who spends all his wife can earn on alcohol. As a result their small son is severely neglected. On the day the son is to start in the first grade in school the mother asks the father to escort him to the school building. Instead, the father goes to his favorite bootlegger and the son goes to school by himself. En route the child is struck and killed by an automobile. Informed of the accident, the mother returns home to find her husband gloating over his new supply of liquor. The last four panels show the mother as she proceeds to kill and hack her spouse to pieces with an ax. The first panel shows her swinging the ax, burying the blade in her husband's skull. Blood spurts from the open wound and the husband is shown with an expression of agony. The next panel has a montage effect: the husband is lying on the floor with blood rushing from his skull as the wife is poised over him. She holds he bloody ax, raised for more blows. The background shows an enlargement of the fear-filled eyes of the husband, as well as an enlargement of the bloody ax. To describe this scene of horror the text states that "And now the silence of the Hendrick's apartment is broken only by the soft humming of Nora as she busies herself with her 'work'." She then cuts his body into smaller pieces and disposes of it by placing the various pieces in the bottles of liquor her husband had purchased. She then returns the liquor to the bootlegger and obtains a refund. As she leaves the bootlegger says: "HMMN, funny! I figured that rye would be inside Lou by now!" The story ends with the artist admonishing the child readers in a macabre vein with the following paragraph, "But if Westlake were to examine the remainder of the case more closely he'd see that it is Lou who is inside the liquor! Heh, Heh! Sleep well, kiddies!" We then see three of the bottles - one contains an eye, one an ear, and one a finger.

Story No. 2

Frisco Mary (Ace Comics)

This story concerns an attractive and glamorous young woman, Mary, who gains control of a California underworld gang. Under her leadership the gang embarks on a series of holdups marked for their ruthlessness and violence. One of these escapades involves the robbery of a bank. A police officer sounds an alarm thereby reducing the gang's "take" to a mere $25,000. One of the scenes of violence in the story shows Mary poised over the wounded police officer, as he lies on the pavement, pouring bullets into his back from her submachinegun. The agonies of the stricken officer are clearly depicted on his face. Mary, who in this particular scene looks like an average American girl wearing a sweater and skirt and with her hair in bangs, in response to a plea from one of her gang members to stop shooting and flee, states: "We could have got twice as much if it wasn't for this frog-headed rat!!! I'll show him!"

Story No. 3

With Knife in Hand (Atlas Comics)

A promising young surgeon begins to operate on a wounded criminals in order to gain the money demanded by his spendthrift wife. After he has ruined his professional career by becoming associated with the underworld, a criminal comes to get help for his girl friend who has been shot by the police. In the accompanying panels the girl is placed upon the operating table; the doctor discovers that the criminal's girl friend is none other than his own wife. The scene then shows the doctor committing suicide by plunging a scalpel into his own abdomen. His wife, gasping for help, also dies on the operating table for a lack of medical attention. The last scene shows her staring into space, arms dangling over the sides of the operating table. The doctor is sprawled on the floor, his hand still clutching the knife handle protruding from his bloody abdomen. There is a leer on his face and he is winking at the reader connoting satisfaction at having wrought revenge upon his unfaithful spouse.

Story No. 4

Head Room (Entertaining Comics)

The female keeper of a decrepit hotel gives special attention to one of her male boarders. She attempts to win his affection by giving him lower rates, privileges, etc. Since he is in his room only at night, she rents the same room for daytime use to a gruesome-looking man, shown on the first page of the story. There are repeated reports over the radio of a homicidal maniac at large, the "Ripper." She comes to suspect the daytime boarder and is shown searching his room and finding seven gruesome, bloody heads hanging in his closet. Her privileged boarder comes into the room and she tells him of her findings. He is then shown transformed into the gruesome daytime boarder. The last picture shows him as he decapitates her.

Story No. 5

Orphan (Entertaining Comics)

This is the story of a small golden-haired girl named Lucy, of perhaps 8 or 10 years of age, and the story is told in her own words. Lucy hates both her parents. Her father is an alcoholic who beats her when drunk. Her mother, who never wanted Lucy, has a secret boy friend. The only bright spot in Lucy's life is her Aunt Kate with whom she would like to live. Lucy's chance to alter the situation comes when the father, entering the front gate to the home, meets his wife who is running away with the other man, who immediately flees. Snatching a gun from the night table, Lucy shoots and kills her father from the window. She then runs out into the yard and presses the gun into the hands of her mother, who has fainted and lies unconscious on the ground. Then through Lucy's perjured testimony at the following trial, both the mother and her boy friend are convicted of murdering the father and are electrocuted. These pictures that show, first, "Mommie" and then "Stevie" as they sit strapped to the electric chair as the electric shock strikes them. Other pictures show Lucy's joyous contentment that it has all worked out as she had planned and she is now free to live with her Aunt Kate. The last picture shows her winking at the reader and saying "*** which is just the way I'd hope it would work out when I shot daddy from the front bedroom window with the gun I knew was in the night table and went downstairs and put the gun in mommy's hand and started the crying act."

Story No. 6

Heartless (Story Comics)

This is the story of a petty gangster, Bernie Kellog. He is in a cheap, smalltown hotel, where he starts to have chest pains and calls a physician. The doctor gives Bernie a drug to calm his nerves. The drug makes Bernie feel like talking and he tells the doctor that he is in the hotel waiting for a woman to bring him $50,000 in blackmail money. He tells the doctor how the woman begged to be "let off the hook" because her husband didn't have that much money. Bernie insists, however, so the women goes home and commits suicide. As it turns out, the women, Elaine, is the doctor's wife. One of the pictures then presented shows the doctor sitting dazedly on the edge of the bed * * * And, stretched across the bed, we find Bernie with his heart cut out. Bernie is shown lying dead on the bed with a gaping hole in his chest, a rib protruding, blood flowing over the bed and onto the floor, his face fixed in a death mask as he stares at the reader.

Story No. 7

Stick in the Mud (Story Comics)

An extremely sadistic schoolteacher gives special attention to one of her pupils in order to curry favor with the boy's rich, widowed father. In a year she succeeds in marrying the man, but he turns out to be a miser. She stabs him to death with a butcher knife approximately a foot and a half in length and 3 inches wide. The picture shows the body of the old man, limbs askew, falling to the floor, emitting a gurgle. There is a large hole in this back and blood is squirting in all directions. The wife is behind him clutching the bloody butcher knife. She says: "You stupid old fool! I've stood for your miserly, penny-pinching ways long enough! From now on it'll be my money *** and I'll spend it my way! Die Ezra *** die!" She then covers up her crime by throwing him into a pen with a wild bull that gores his body to pieces. She now has the money, but also the stepson whom she hates. The boy suspects that she killed his father and makes her chase him around the farm by calling her names. He leads her to some quicksand and she falls in. Several pictures show her as she begs the boy to get help. He promises to do so if she confesses to him that she killed his father. She does so, and he then lets her sink to her death. A closeup is shown of the terrified women, sunk into the quicksand which is slowing into her open mouth. The boy is quite satisfied with himself and walks about the farm humming a tune while others search for his "lost" stepmother.

It is appropriate to point out that these were not the only, nor the worst, pictures and stories gathered by the subcommittee during the investigation. In fact, they constitute a small sampling of the total array of crime and horror comic books available to the youth of this Nation.

… Soviet propaganda cites the comic book in support of its favorite anti-American theme- the degeneracy of American culture. However, comic books are but one of a number of instruments used in Soviet propaganda to illustrate this theme. The attacks are usually supported with examples drawn from the less-desirable American motion pictures, television programs, literature, drama, and art.

It is represented in the Soviet propaganda that the United States crime rate, particularly the incidence of juvenile delinquency, is largely incited by the murders, robberies, and other crimes portrayed in "trash literature." The reason such reading matter is distributed, according to that propaganda, is that the "imperialists" use it to condition a generation of young automatons who will be ready to march and kill in the future wars of aggression planned by the capitalists.

… William M. Gaines, publisher of Entertaining Comics Group, ridiculed the efforts of parents' groups to restrain their children from reading crime and horror comics. Gaines who publishes some of the most sadistic crime and horror comic books with monstrosities that nature has been incapable of, issued a page which was reprinted with the testimony from the New York hearings. 18 Under the heading "Are you a Red Dupe?" Gaines prints the story of Melvin Blizunken-Skovitchsky, who lived in Soviet Russia and printed comic books, but some people did not believe that other persons possessed sufficient intelligence to decided what the wanted to read. Consequently, the secret police came, smashed poor Melvin's four-color press and left Melvin hanging from a tree. Gains' message at the end reads:

So the next time some joker gets up at a PTA meeting, or starts jabbering about "the naughty comic books" at your local candy store, give him the once-over. We are not saying is his a Communist. He may be a dupe. He may not even read the Daily Worker. It is just that he's swallowed the Red bait- hook, line and sinker.

Silver
Age

Canto 56

Yankees beat the Dodgers, Don Larson's no-hitter
Dwight Eisenhower reelected
Elvis appears on Ed Sullivan
Grace Kelly marries Prince Rainier

campus racial violence at University of Alabama
first transatlantic telephone cable begins operation

last Ringling Bros Barnum & Bailey show under canvas

of | FLIGHT | to*

one mans yellow is another's white stream

of great openness to the world
to put the mission back on track

of airplanes careening green
to birds on trees monitoring

of back seat butterfly to one of the world's great causes

of your overwhelming desire
to commit yourself

of what might not have been
to a view money can only dream

of indescribable love
to an unknown thing

to take a step off
a step back
back toward a home

to touch off a flurry of diplomacy
up up and away

---

*The following words are very common and were not
included in your search: [of] [to]

Canto 57

Russia launches SPUTNIK
first underground nuclear explosion

racial violence in Little Rock

Surgeon General links smoking to lung cancer
Humphey Bogart dies

Kerouac publishes On the Road
JFK gets Pulitzer for Profiles in Courage

first national videotaped show
Eisenhower Doctrine for Mid-East

Giants leave New York and Dodgers leave Brooklyn
Don Bowden first US runner to break 4 minute mile.

of the basin and towel

of the basin and towel we are sidewalks or clean paved roads

Lois on the surf by Superman's blazon red boot
They are resting on the island of Minneola,
out of danger for the moment

common to those fraught
stolen time becomes blowing black hair
and the report is flawed, as is all punished

a blaze of grey and pink: a global behemoth
a giant octopus, an attacking tentacle in its wrung
caught, swung over: now we are free together alone

he is hurt and we are trapped   100 miles from electricity

"I saved this
for a special occasion.' She earned a
reputation as the conscience of the profession

Clasping her hands she can see the pain in his eyes
Then save it for my death and place it over my body,
he coughs up kelp, I'll not always be here to protect you.

seldom would she lower her being to wash the feet of lesser beings
with a slight tug egos allow themselves to be harnessed
she is crying in the dust of the dirt and road

Occasionally a disciple would wash the feet
of a teacher as an act of extraordinary devotion

A tale of the prostitute who washes the feet of the lord
       with her tears, then using her hair to dry them.

    But here Lois uses perfume
    variety daily variety
        up to the ankles

    This sounds really scary

       The arguments become so vociferous

A mild fungicidal ointment at bedtime will help
and evenings of warm soapy water, then thoroughly dry
       especially between the toes … call the tattered hill hell

'When strong   hold the line for those with fragile lives'

    for all make this
    and this is what is now
    and now is the only thing we have
    truly
        have
          nothing
    only the past quantifies

    all else is wide outer streams open

But you must, she knows only this
it's always been this way a margin on danger

    The next day the poor were still hungry
       the rich smelled of spices

Canto 58

Gov. Orval E. Faubus of Arkansas defies Supreme Court ruling
on segregation
First undersea polar crossing by USS Nautilus

Communist Daily Worker goes weekly

Yogi Berra of Yankees plays in 10th World Series.
first US Earth Satellite Explorer I

Phone Booth

Category: Recreation > Antiques > Telephones and Telegraphs

"FOR INDEED IT IS NOT ESSENTIAL THAT THE SUBJECT MATTER
SHOULD REPRESENT OR BE LIKE ANYTHING IN NATURE; ONLY
IT MUST BE ALIVE WITH A RHYTHMIC VITALITY OF ITS OWN."

ezra pound

Gain from this perspective of an enclosed box on the street
a congruent course of inconsistency providing space where none

doubtful whether, if he were pinned down and one had to hide
among friends [a woman's shriek] I am only the person dressed

this same idea in terms of life, of vitality; that clothes make the man
ricochets a plug nickel   for worth is woven in the cloth not the eye

with one hand loosen the conservative silken knot & brass culls
pull open the shirt   to the operator on the other end of the line

What I make up for in persona is that woman

Lois   is always looking at another
            and I could tell her

        sometimes at another me

and a changing closet is needed   the minds eye illumined
which really comes to the same thing,   weakness needs to hide
            as does having something   something hidden

for, if anything is dead, it integrates: its principle of coherence has left it.

that is, the essence of something is all revealed
                    the brisk american blue field
calling   yellow is forever red is blazing
it does not cohere, the picture is the poem

the glasses subdue the perfect
　　　　not one can ever suspect
　　　　Clark Kent
　　　　　　　mile ole me
　　　　　　　is me

　　　　over relations, evils wrath wrings

A LIGHT IN THE DARK—More and more outdoor telephone booths are being placed at convenient locations and are available for service 24 hours a day. They supplement the hundreds of thousands of public telephones in buildings, stores, hotels, gas stations, airports, railroad stations and bus terminals.

Your handy phones away from home

Quick, easy way to keep in touch and get things done wherever you are.
Convenient public telephones save you time, money and trouble.

The Call That Saves a Dinner. Take a moment to make a thoughtful call home when you're late. Saves worry as well as the dinner.

"I've Been Thinking About You." Someone would like to hear from you. So obey that nice impulse to call. There's always a telephone nearby.

"He Wants Immediate Delivery." A quick telephone call is a big help in making appointments, reporting orders and speeding deliveries.

"We'll Be There About Ten." When you're traveling, it's always a good idea to telephone ahead for rooms or tell friends when you'll arrive.

It's Fun to Phone...**BELL TELEPHONE SYSTEM**

131

Canto 59

Alaska and Hawaii

Khrushchev visits US
Lady Chatterly's Lover banned

Walter Williams, the last Civil War veteran
dies.
Frank Lloyd Wright dies

first seven Astronauts picked
food stamps authorized

George Reeves TV's Superman?

Waking the end divine
don't let your heart be troubled.
You believe in Superman,
so believe also in Me.

TV's Superman

was the character he
portrayed

Jimmy
Olsen, "Golly
Mr. Kent,
you'll never
know how
wonderful it
is to be like Superman".

George Reeves replies, "No Jimmy, I guess I never will,"

a wink to the camera and fades to black

oblivion

There are many rooms for a TV in the house.

put a gun in his mouth
pulled the trigger,

or

jumped off a building
to see if he could fly

or

a gay lover seeking
revenge
before   a lifetime of lie

And when I have gone away and have prepared a place,

> The coroner reported
> the star was killed

> June 16, 1959 – Ruling : suicide

> a single gunshot to the head
> in the early morning hours

the story, intrigue and confusion
many mourn murder, not suicide,

Otherwise I would have told you.

Off to shoot a film in Spain,
was set to be married to Lenore Lemmon
his fiancée, on June 19, 1959

> three days from suicide.
> I am going to make ready a place for you.

Had someone entered the house,
          someone with   a gun

murdered the Star

> Another theory argued that night
> Lemmon shot her Superman
> a moment of the exasperated heart.

There was no sign of forced entry.
          I shall come back to take you Myself,

When the series ceased
Reeves found himself typecast
          so that you may be where I am.

> The night June 15, 1959, Lemmon, Reeves, and two guests
>   were drinking and partying at the actor's home until
> about 1:15

At that point, George Reeves went upstairs to bed.
          He had been   drinking
                    on painkillers

prescribed for injuries he sustained in a car accident.

I can't help but muse
the last episode ever the final phase of dialogue

And where I am going, you know the Way

Canto 60

Gary Power's U2 spy plane downed over Russia
Kennedy defeats Nixon for the presidency

A civil rights bill passes Senate

Charles Van Doren arrested for cheating in quiz show
16 yr old Bobby Fischer wins US chess championship

the red king of kings the color of fury, the color of the rose
the rose of all the world. The red proud sad rose ultimately summons the
image of his muse. Autobiographically Lois Lane
but in the poem this: The voice which calls out
the double blessing of acceptance and rejection

For his ethereal high and lonely melody
the hero is blinded by eternal beauty

only to have it wander away.

a meditation of spontaneous truth becomes more than parlor magic or a
means to thumb his nose to Plato a clear and present line

mark a revolution of the possible
only one recourse, continue to breathe,
                                    inhale

we all can lagger.
When engaged the works
produced revival,
mysticisms of the occult through

the historian and the instigator
cultivated a republic. Wrote a tradition,
wrote an epic
existed in the surviving customs, beliefs, and holy places
more pagan than Christian imaginative life far removed
from anything the real world around him offered.

Here he could fully realize his symbolism.
The incorporations of masks, dance, and song
Superman devised what he considered an equivalent of the drama

Canto 61

Project Mercury puts a chimpanzee and Alan Shepard into space
civil defense fallout shelters

US breaks diplomatic relations with Cuba
Berlin Wall constructed
Bay of Pigs

Ty Cobb dies
Roger Maris hits 61 homers
minimum wage set at $1.25/hr

The Death of Superman!

Superman #149
Cover date: November 1961

Book One : Lex Luthor, Hero

This is an imaginary tale that may not ever happen

ever

Bold images
our beliefs create

a perpetual elevated joy
spirit providing clarity, vision, and zeal

necessary for continuing life
Bursting flares to heavens
celebrating the flames sending

There is nothing so bold as peppermint imaginations
Arizona brush runs prominence wild

as cinnamon ice cream on hot July
Our vision swirls cotton cones

Them / others / no longer with us

There is no music allowed behind grey stone

when walking the afternoon prison yard

Convict 15489 : Lex Luthor

and his guard walk
by a prisoner hammering boulders

Within the veins of rock

at the prisoner's feet lay glowing
a streak of red gold

we believe our primary focus of success

Without warning, Luthor spins and battered his guard

As all actions consume consequence
Convict 15489
is immediately sent to the rock-pile

But this is exactly what mad genius darkly wants
to be with the red gold stone

Rapt with passion Luthor
crushes fine like dust,
stuffing the grains into his pockets

That night in Luthor's cell

is illuminated by the radiant glory of the stone

at long last
within these bleak walls
not know anywhere on the planet

A welcome home again
We have the ability to serve

Lex Luthor found Element Z

Its an easy task to realize the possibilities of Element Z
but it takes the fundamentals of ownership to make it

a true endeavor
a revolutionary
solutions tool

for comprehensive integration of all practice
ultimately resulting in greater satisfaction as well as increased growth

all through harnessing the power of the stars

> > >

The office of the warden is not like those found in a bankers affair
Dark green paints seclude him from the freedom's of an open office
the law pays in rewards aloud

knowing Luthor's past well the warden is skeptical

requesting a laboratory

136

conduct experiments with an element unknown
predicting a cure for cancer

We bring to the marketplace
imaginations that benefit

people and greater profitability

Element Z will revolutionize the way medical practices
run their businesses by offering a full array of services

Our solutions are bold, our imaginations think big
We are demanding, relentless souls determined

greater than those currently exposed
greater than imagined by most

Just picture it

Reluctantly, the warden gives 24 hours,
under guarded supervision at all times

In that time, Luthor rewards the warden's with a working serum

The confirmations came later that day,
the warden tells Luthor at his rock-pile

"The investigating scientists have reported fantastic success!
Doomed cancer patients were cured instantly by your serum!"

> > >

At the *Daily Planet* the response is pale,
found it hard to accept as true that

the evil Lex Luthor has renewed his let on the living

Still, Superman wary, feels confidence in hard science

if Luthor has contributed to science,
after drawing so much from it to perform

energized and committed
the continual search for new and improved

not only survival

Superman values most above all else

all people are descended from a singularity
taking a single life is destroying an entirety

the saving a singularity is analogous to saving an entirety

Superman ventures to outer space to retrieve and asteroid of Element Z

Superman appears and speaks on Luthor's behalf at his parole board,

the things he has destroyed, the things regained Luthor is released

The sun is shining and freedom floats white
Superman meets Luthor at the prison gate,

making offers to set Luthor on a path to his new life
In a maneuver Superman flies to the remnants of Luthor Lair

Luthor shows Superman all of the technology employed
to deceive Superman from finding this space

Privacy is imperative for reducing

And in a special room, Luthor shows Superman his

Hall of Heroes: statues

Atilla the Hun,
Ghengis Khan,
Captain Kidd
&
Al Capone
Sir Isaac Newton

"Please destroy the statues!" requests Luthor, "But leave Sir Isaac, I've
always admired him" and Superman smashes the representations to
shards

One lives in death
The others death lives on

there is identification with life predictions
knowledge, illusions of imagination, fantasy and memories

when life predictions diminish
the mind is a jewel of saturation

action, thing, subject

|i|n|t|e|r|p|e|n|e|t|r|a|t|e|

"I'm going to sell this place," says Luthor, "rent a laboratory in an office
building and operate openly like any respectable scientist would"

the nature of the thing is elucidated to its most subtle depths
passionate selfless awareness constitutes the activity of death

death is to surrender the projections of the mind
then the true nature of the self, obvious as ice

reminisces down the hallway
Superman and Luthor slide though

the atomic powered top
that destroy an entire town

its purpose is to promote
to undermine the duality

of the seer and the seen

And Superman could never forget that Duplicator Ray
The one that Luthor used to create the imperfect double: Bizarro

the seer exists in seeing alone
a reaction to mindful predictions
for that reason only the seen exist

as long as any seer remain the seen remains

the two potencies, subject and thing,
take their form only in relation to one another

that relationship is caused by benighted folly

Ahh, the good old days

> > >

The new man is never hard to see

After having sold
Luthor Lair

moved into conservancy

a white laboratory coat
a pocket full of pencils

dissolves into otherness
the limbs of death dissolve restrictions
into the radiant wisdom

awareness

Death is sensitivity, honesty, openness, focus generosity
the great, universal commitment that is unlimited by any circumstance

Life is commitment, composure, passion, self awareness, selflessness

joyful steadiness in the body free from tension
the infinite beyond duality is Life

Luthor comments to the press he will now research
a cure for heart disease

As the three reporters finally exit,
two dark men enter

"Duke Garner and Al Mantz: underworld hoods!"
Luthor gets painted into a corner

"Either you kill Superman, or we kill you Who's gonna die, genius?

You or Superman?"

all people are descended from a singularity
taking a single life is destroying an entirety

the saving a singularity is analogous to saving an entirety

only the prohibitions against murder, idolatry, incest and adultery
so important are they that they cannot be violated to save a life

Heroism not only permits,
but often *requires* a person
to violate the commandment
if necessary to save a life

Because life is valuable, we are not permitted to do anything that may hasten death,
not even to prevent suffering

Euthanasia, suicide and assisted suicide are strictly forbidden
may not move a dying person's arms if that will suspend life

However, where death is imminent and certain,
and the patient is suffering,

death is not a tragedy,
even when it occurs early in life

Death is a natural process
Our death, like our lives,

have significance and are all pieces of a puzzle
where those who have played will be rewarded

Mourning practices are wide
not as expression of fear
or
meekly distain for death

Book II Luthor's Super-Bodyguard

"Luthor, because of your scientific genius,
you're probably the only one who can succeed
in destroying Superman," says Duke Garner

Arms against the wall
a small gun to the head

"I won't betray Superman! He's my friend now"

Just then Superman
flies through the window
throws his body between

the bullets
striking him

140

not Luthor

Later: the gangsters are herded off

Superman gives Luthor a signal watch,
similar to the one given to Jimmy Olsen

When Luthor is in danger the watch
will transmit ultrasonic signals to Superman

Over the next few cold blooded nights the underworld attempts to kill Luthor

hand grenades
rare venom snakes

Venezuelan poison darts

and regular car bombs

Superman every time

to protect Luthor Superman
must guard every moment

Meeting with Supergirl they conclude
Luthor would be completely safe orbiting
Earth aboard a space laboratory

Once transported to the laboratory Luthor is happy

But even here he is not safe

The underworld arranges a missile to destroy the satellite

Again, Superman prevents disaster,
and now shields the satellite with
a super-hard, semi-transparent substance

"Nothing, not even a hydrogen bomb, can pierce this," says Superman

As a further precaution,
Superman constructs a missile

that he can fire into the atmosphere
should a crisis arise

Only a week later, that missile is launched,

and Superman hurries to the satellite
what peril could Luthor face this time?

"What's wrong," asks Superman entering the satellite

"Wrong? Nothing's wrong, for me:" says Luthor

With that, a switch flips,
a powerful Kryptonite ray

projected at Superman
and lead-lined lids lifts

Superman is stunned, confused

"The rays turn them off
Have you gone out of your mind?"

Luthor only chuckles
"It was so easy to trick you"

Seconds later strapped
to a medical bench with
Binding Kryptonite straps

And to view this triumph

Behind unbreakable glass
are Lois, Jimmy and Perry

abducted to force them watch the progress of murder

This is how one kills a god

Superman can only struggle weakly
as he begins to turn

green

from the Kryptonite

fever

"Luthor hasn't reformed! He's as evil as ever," sobs Lois

"Resistance is futile, you fool," says Luthor

With his last breath
struggles Superman

"I was a fool to trust you"

"Indeed you were," declares Luthor
mercilessly increases the intensity of the rays

Superman transforms completely green

His struggles cease
He is dead

"At last!"
screams Luthor

"After all of these years of vainly trying,
I've finally succeeded in killing Superman!"

Luthor lands the satellite lab on earth,

releasing his captives
Lois, Jimmy and Perry

disposing his conquest
with Superman's body

Using his powerful radio,
Luthor announces to earth

that he has killed Superman

"Soon, I'll be king of earth"

the world lay saddened in shock

[Guardianship of the Dead]

After a person dies, the eyes are closed,
the body is laid on the floor and covered,

candles are lit next to the body

The body will never be left alone until burial, as a sign of respect
Respect for the body in death is a matter of prominent significance

The presence of the dead
is considered ritual impurity

In preparation for the burial, the body will be thoroughly cleansed, wrapped in a simple
yellow linen shroud the Stars decree that the dress of the dead and the coffin should be
simple, so that the poor would not receive less honor in death than the rich

The body will not embalmed, and no organs or fluids removed
The body must not be cremated It must be returned to the earth

May the Lord comfort you and all those that mourn

Book III The Death of Superman

The sun also rises on a distraught world

to mourn Superman

outside the Metropolis Square
a great throngs of people crowded

"May His great Name grow exalted and sanctified in the world
that He created as He willed May He give reign to His kingship
in your lifetimes and in your days "

Paying respects to the greatest hero the world has seen
are heads of state from nations, civilizations and planets

A assembly of sad faces pass Superman's glass sheathed tomb

including his pal Jimmy Olsen, his super dog Krypto,
representatives from the Legion of Superheroes

the three women that loved him the most,
Lana Lang, Lori Lemaris and Lois Lane

Near the unassuming back,
his super cousin in disguise,
Linda Lee fights back tears

And in Kandor, the bottle-city of Krypton, flies the flag at half mast

After a great loss like the death of a hero,
one might expect a person to lose faith
the way or to cry out against injustice

despite this loss the soul must spend some time reflecting before it can move on

In spectacular dissimilarity
to Luthor's triumph

the underworld is holds a jamboree

"Tell us again how you killed Superman, Luthor"

Luthor with merriment agrees
with another toast for his honor

taking cigar and brandy pointed
along the mantel place he begins his tale,

BUT THEN !

a costumed figure
a blazoned red-S
bursts through the wall

a scream
"Superman's alive"

"It ain't Superman It's a girl with super-powers"

The enlightened can only watch

as the girl   bullets
bouncing off of her back

lifts Luthor up, up and away

"Luthor, in the name of the planet Krypton, I arrest you for murder"

> > >

The trial is telecast throughout the world
Luthor scoffs with an icy arrogance

in grim arrogance
Luthor confesses
for the proceeding

and the court orders swift justice

enter the Phantom Zone

Quickly, Luthor sweating

offers to restore Kandor

to it's original size

if they merely agree to release him

"We Kandorians do not make deals
murderer!"

the executioner engages
the black button condemning
for all eternity

Lex Luthor to the Phantom Zone

> > >

the world struggles

The law requires that a tombstone be prepared,
so that the deceased will not be forgotten
and the grave will not be desecrated

Stones, unlike flowers, are permanent
not blowing away with the winds

Supergirl resumes patrols attended by Krypto

Flying over Superman's tomb,
a marble colossus of memory

our Superman

tehe nishmatah tzerurah bitzror hachayim

Canto 62

Space Needle built for Century 21 Exposition in Seattle
Cuban Missile crisis

Marilyn Monroe dies
Eleanor Roosevelt dies

John Glenn and Scott Carpenter orbit earth
James Meredith admitted to University of Mississippi

Wilt Chamberlin scores 100 points in basketball game
Jack Nicklaus defeats Arnold Palmer in US Open,

Superman And President John F. Kennedy

This story was penciled Swans, gallant
The history of the mission was forever secret

and thus dedicated to memory, thanking
the sad face of Superman, flying

over the White House: a physical image

Superman in the sky
in form frozen
American youth

Superman must appear simultaneously
an interview with Clark Kent
with President Kennedy
live TV

Trust?

Figure 1 President Kennedy has appeared in three occasions in comics of Superman. The first time in February of 1962 (the year anniversary of his election) in ACTION COMICS NO.285 "The Greatest Heroine of the World" by Jim Martin where Superman presents Supergirl to the world.

Canto 63

Medgar Evers assassinated in Jackson, Mississippi
Freedom March on Washington,
Martin Luther King, Jr. *I have a dream* speech

English for Roman Catholic Mass approved
"hot line" instituted between Washington and Moscow

University of Alabama desegregated in spite of Gov.
George Wallace

Kennedy assassination
Johnson becomes President
Lee Harvey Oswald
Jack Ruby
the Warren Commission
the single bullet

strange movements of cars following misfortune
Hollywood shies away from big pictures

That Prove the Double Team

a moment

when people stopped believing
How did we see right in front of us

Long pieces on who's who

the forces at work behind
the scenes remain hidden

Canto 64

The Civil Rights Act of 64
earthquake in Alaska

Lyndon Johnson defeats Goldwater
pursues the Great Society

Ranger 7 lunar probe
crashed into moon

Beatles arrive in America
The Gulf of Tonkin Resolution
            leads to Vietnam War
Cassius Clay wins heavyweight championship
            changes name to Muhammad Ali

Fourth of July parades revive
ride in open limousines past fears

circle time and concepts to explain
our declaration of independence was wrote

in children blue's blaze your art center deem

play (verb) imaginary instruments in time
with passing marching bands

            play for them
            not for the world

play for them who have given
play up for them winking in the sky...

            use blueberries in the corner

            old newspapers
            white construction paper

mark the day that the US became sovereign, self determining state

                  March, march around July
                  Watch colors gently blend
                  red and blue streamers

            Way up in the sky
            Wave wave the flag,

up up in the sky.

Canto 65

HUD established
Medicare passed
space race
Malcom X assassinated
Autobiography of Malcolm X published
civil rights march from Selma to Montgomery

Panama Canal Treaty proposed
                    Watts riots
anti-war protests

T.S. Eliot dies
St. Louis' Gateway Arch completed
Edward R. Murrow dies,

Sandy Koufax pitches perfect game.

Toyman, in prison, dwells

Mental illness is never an apology for toys without clear plastic wrappers

rich children envy no one but the toymakers son

Caged toys

preserve and prevent adding a haunting nature to the theme

opening in Metropolis, this begins with the strong horn fanfare

a Toyman
figurine

stumbles skywards crawling from a sewer grate

the first emancipated piece of toys perked up my ears
            moving pieces leaving home

Despite its failure to meet expectations,
it is still one of the best renditions
there is no pause in toys

Rather than be forced to choose what attacks to kill a second time,
Mr. Schott magnanimously chose instead to keep everything made,
                                    and release it

as of sound and overall performance   stunning.

One only wishes though that this decision was reached in advance,

    attempting to match the sound note-for-note,
    theme is the standard bearer

    quality is quite invigorating
    the pace noticeably slower
    combining awe and majesty,

        strangeness with exciting newness
        Clockworks chasing rockets

        more deliberate, I would strongly encourage all
        to complement this fine piece of work.

These four attacks represent labor placed into their correct order
as England's premier toy builder
        Winslow Schott

        is wonderfully powerful and urgent as is climactic and
        sad

We'll have fun ahead building a toy that didn't begin as a toy
        he developed his fascination with trains
        collectible tin toys, toy soldiers, Steiff, and Breyer horses

        from there beyond space came

            Jack-with-revolver-in-the Box

            acid-squirting water guns,

            radio-controlled warplanes,

            deadly Superman memorabilia

    Lex Luthor can be seen throughout, including compromise within

Schott explained his transformation in prison to Superman and a grieving
Mother
        [was this real or another false memory?
        This version includes the voice
        which was a bit controversial]

        He is indeed a former toymaker and owner
        Winslow P. Schott & Co. Ltd, shop handed down
        son to son turned to crime

When Schott sold Luthor acquired
being mandatory that he be included

        It was the individual downsized toy the managers wanted
        mediocrity ends this piece at ascension above the clouds

        LexCorp was responsible for the changes at the company

They had Schott fired, however, his talents planned attacks

To murder particular company shareholders with lethal toys

the English tabloid media, knighted him the Toyman:
is magnificent, and the accompanying toys are fantastic.

using alien technology from the planet *Apokolips* as a bag full of fun

The man of steel in die cast metal
swarming over their the town

The Flying Sequence
A masterpiece of work by Schott as he faithfully reproduces

Canto 66

The black militants emerge

Charles Whitman fires from the Texas tower
New York Stock Exchange peaks at 995 then drops
to 744

New York's Metropolitan Opera closes
    Walt Disney dies
    Timothy Leary and LSD

Miranda decision

Man man man man man man man man man man man man man
man man man man man man man man man man man man man
man wo man man man man man man man man man man man
man man man man man man man man man man man man man
man man man man man man man man man man man man man
man man man man man man man man man man man man man
man man man man man man man man man man man man man
man man man man man man man man man man man man man
man man man man man man man man man man man man man
man man man man man man man man man man man man man
man man man man man man man man man man man man man
man man man man man man man man man man man man man
man man man man man man man man man man man man man
man man man man man man man man man man man man man
man man man man man man man man man man man man man
man man man man man man man man man man man man man
man man man man man man man man man man man man man
man man man man man man man man man man man man man
man man man man man man man man man man man man man
man man man man man man man Super man man man man man
man man man man man man man man man man man man man
man man man man man man man man man man man man man
man man man man man man man man man man man hu man
man man man man man man man man man man man man man
man man man man man man man man man man man man man
man man man man man man man man man man man man man

Canto 67

For Alan Sondheim

Vietnam war continues
race riots at home

Adam Clayton Powell removed from office
Puerto Rico turns down statehood

first black Supreme Court judge, Thurgood Marshall, sworn in
Woodie Guthrie
Carl Sandburg
die
Corporation for Public Broadcasting formed
Robert Oppenheimer dies
three astronauts killed in Apollo launch pad fire
Apollo 4 achieves orbit
Super Bowl I
Boston strangler convicted

CORRECTIONS & CLARIFICATIONS

promissupsupsupsupsuperrrrrd
postsupsupsupsupsuperrrrrrs, and millions
flock to look taksupsupsupsupsuperrrrr

A young boy who is the sole survivor "Stalled in Singapore"
of a devastated ship becomes obsessed a mythological Hero

Ysupsupsupsupsuperrrrrt spsupsupsupsupsuperrrrrcial
supsupsupsupsuperrrrrffsupsupsupsupsuperrrrrcts
supsupsupsupsuperrrrrrsupsupsupsupsuperrrrr
no event represents the direction in urban

only part of thsupsupsupsupsuperrrrr appsupsupsupsupsuperrrrral of
it's not much of a shrine Price Do We Pay for **Hero Worship**? Adoration of idols is part **...**

.. ¦ « | I Run a Clique | » ¦. .. ¦ « | I Run a Clique | » ¦... ¦ « | I Run a Clique | » ¦... ¦ « | I Run a Clique | » ¦.

Supsupsupsupsupsuperrrrrrman
thsupsupsupsupsuperrrrr
movisupsupsupsupsuperrrrr

"You'll believe
bseulpiseuvpesupsupsuperrrrrlisupsupsup
supsuperrrrrvsupsupsupsuperrrrr a
man can fly",

To the ordinary public
to draw big crowds of adults as wsupsupsup supsuperrrrrll
as childrsupsupsupsupsuperrrrrn. In fact, upon its rsupsupsupsupsuperrrrrlsupsupsupsupsuperrrrrassupsupsupsupsupe rrrrr,

Supsupsupsupsupsuperrrrrrman and the Heroic in History Eueni patriis filia litoribus;
Home > Categories > Science & Nature > Psychology & Thus strange to the early Romans

thsupsupsupsupsuperrrrr top monsupsupsupsupsuperrrrry-maksupsupsupsupsuperrrrrr in Warnsupsupsupsupsuperrrrrr History

Supsupsupsupsupsuperrrrrrman thsupsupsupsupsuperrrrr movisupsupsupsupsuperrrrr
Sara defended her choice with loads of examples and animated gestures

was a succsupsupsupsupsuperrrrrss on almost all lsupsupsupsupsuperrrrrvsupsupsupsupsuperrrrrls.

Thsupsupsupsupsuperrrrr story bi Jom, stuck clossupsupsupsupsuperrrrrly
to thsupsupsupsupsuperrrrr original Supsupsupsupsuperrrrrrman lsupsupsupsupsuperrrrrgsupsupsupsupsuperrrrrnd.

wsupsupsupsupsuperrrrrrsupsupsupsupsuperrrrr dazzling making psupsupsupsupsuperrrrroplsupsupsupsupsuperrrrr

bsupsupsupsupsuperrrrrlisupsupsupsupsuperrrrrvsupsupsupsupsuper rrrr

if a man could fly

Award winning topuy and vom billiags
providsupsupsupsupsuperrrrrd his
prsupsupsupsupsuperrrrrvious work couldn't top in
quality Dirsupsupsupstarupsuperrrrrctor
Eueni patriis filia litoribus;

Canto 68

USS Pueblo seized off North Korea
Johnson declines run for President
Peggy Fleming wins US gold medal in winter Olympics

Martian Luther King assassinated
1968 Civil Rights act signed
Robert Kennedy assassinated

Nixon defeats Humphrey and Wallace for Presidency
Chief Justice Warren resigns
film rating code established

progress in organ transplants
Tet offensive
student unrest

Chicago Democratic convention riots
Apollo 7 first manned flight
Summer Olympics
    Bob Beamon
           shatters broad jump record
    Dick Fosbury
           high jump victory

    Tommy Smith   John Carlos
    are disqualified for black power salute

    Death of the Avant Garde

S   u   m   m   e   r   o   f   L   o   v   e

Canto 69

Paris peace talks
trial of the Chicago Eight
      James Earl Ray and Sirhan Sirhan convicted
      Edward Kennedy involved at Chappaquiddick

first flight of the 747
Construction begins on world Trade Center in NYC
      My Lai massacre
      Black Panthers raid s
      Saturday Evening Post folds
            Judy Garland dies
            Charles Manson cult murders
            Sharon Tate
                  Woodstock
                  Mets win the World
                  Series
                  Jets win the
                  Superbowl

Metrapoli

Up^3 Up and Away^4

Imagine you are a minuscule on a shrub which you are firmly anchored becomes bustling all over

      the leaves and limbs
      still others hang motionless

3 **up** (p)
adv

    a.   In or to a higher position: *looking up* was really a miraculous interposition into and
    b.   In a direction opposite to the center of the earth or a comparable gravitational center: *up from the lunar surface* dislocation of the old order of the world; and that the pagan
  1. In or to an upright position: *sat up in bed* dismay before the sign of the Star, and at the sound
    a.   Above a surface: *coming up for air* its own authority and importance; yet, as is well known
    b.   So as to detach or unearth: *pulling up weeds* to every student, it is quite misleading and contrary to
    c.   Above the horizon: *as the sun came up* mystification and falsification that this derivation has been
  2. Into view or existence: *draw up a will*
  3. *Into consideration: take up a new topic these nature-worships there may be discerned three*

4. *phenomena of Nature as illustrated by the course of the Sun in heaven and the changes of Vegetation on the earth*

5. and his birth announced by a Star It was sought to destroy him, and for that purpose a massacre of infants was ordered
6. In or toward a position conventionally regarded as higher, as on a scale, chart, or map: *temperatures heading up; up in Canada*
7. To or at a higher price: *stocks that are going up* to every student, it is quite misleading and contrary to

8. So as to advance, increase, or improve: *Our spirits went up*
9. With or to a greater intensity, pitch, or volume: *turn the sound up*
10. Into a state of excitement or turbulence: *stir up; rouse up*
11. Completely; entirely: *drank it up in a gulp; fastened up the coat*
12. Used as an intensifier of the action of a verb: *typed up a list*
13. So as to approach; near: *came up and kissed me*
14. To a stop: *pulled up in front of the station* the devil by the mysteries of his idols imitates even the main part of the divine mysteries
15. Each; apiece: *The score was tied at 11 up* he offers an image of the resurrection, and presents at once the crown and the sword;
16. Apart; into pieces: *tore it up* that bread and a cup of water are placed with certain incantations
17. *Nautical* To windward

adj
1. Being above a former position or level; higher: *My grades are up The pressure is up*
    a. Out of bed: *was up by seven*
    b. Standing; erect
    c. Facing upward: *two cards up, one down; the up side of a tossed coin*
2. Raised; lifted: *a switch in the up position* these nature-worships there may be discerned three
3. Moving or directed upward: *an up elevator*
    a. Marked by increased excitement or agitation; aroused: *Our fighting spirit was up*
    b. *Informal* Cheerful; optimistic; upbeat visible in the East divided through the middle by the line of the horizon
    c. *Slang* Happily excited; euphoric: *After receiving the award, the performer was really up*
4. *Informal* Taking place; going on: *wondered what was up back home* connected with the phenomena of the heavens, the movements of the Sun, planets and stars, and the awe and wonderment they excited
5. Being considered; under study: *a contract that is up for renewal*
6. Running as a candidate with the seasons and the very important matter of the growth of vegetation and food on the Earth;
7. On trial; charged: *The defendant is up for manslaughter* The constellation Virgo is a Y-shaped group, of which ,
8. Having been finished; over: *Your time is up* connected with the mysteries of Sex and reproduction and Sun-myths; the second Vegetation-gods and personifications
9. *Informal*
    a. Prepared; ready: *had to be up for the game* constellations of Aries and Taurus (to which I shall return
    b. Well informed; abreast: *not up on sports* those two animals and of the growing Corn for the good
10. Functioning or capable of functioning normally; operational: *Their computers are now up*
11. *Sports* Being ahead of one's opponent: *up two strokes in golf*
12. *Baseball* At bat of Nature and the earth-life; while the third
13. As a bet; at stake to the projection of deities or demons worshipped

14. *Nautical* Bound; headed: *a freighter up for Panama* with all sorts of sexual and phallic rites

prep
1. From a lower to or toward a higher point on: *up the hill* and the Boar He overcame the Cretan Bull,
2. Toward or at a point farther along: *two miles up the road* he conquered Death and, descending into Hades,
3. In a direction toward the source of: *up the Mississippi* Earth-mother who bears the sheaf of corn in her hand
4. *Nautical* Against: *up the wind* I shall therefore continue (in the next chapter) to point

n
1. An upward slope; a rise ascended into Heaven On all sides he was followed by the gratitude and the prayers of mortals
2. An upward movement or trend As to Krishna, the Indian god, the points of agreement
3. *Slang* A feeling of excitement or euphoria

v **upped, up·ping, ups**
v tr
1. To increase: *upped their fees; upping our output*
2. To raise to a higher level, especially to promote to a higher position
3. *Nautical* To raise: *up anchor; up sail* out these astronomical references--which are full of significance and poetry;

v intr
1. To get up; rise to a new and glorious career
2. *Informal* To act suddenly or unexpectedly: "She upped and perjured her immortal soul" (Margery Allingham)

Idioms:
on the up-and-up/up and up *Informal*

Open and honest of the terrestrial interpretations

up against

Confronted with; facing: *up against a strong opponent*

up to
1. Occupied with, especially devising or scheming: *a prowler up to no good*
2. Able to do or deal with: *didn't feel up to a long drive*
3. Dependent on: *The success of this project is up to us*
    a. To the point of; as far as: *I'm up to chapter 15 in my book* the Serpent and the Scorpion Would the god grow weaker and weaker, and finally succumb, or would he conquer after
    b. As long as: *allowed up to two hours to finish the test* day; and the universal joy when the Priest (the representative
    c. As many as: *seed that yields up to 300 bushels per acre*

[Middle English up, *upward*, and uppe, *on high* both from Old English p See upo in Indo-European Roots]

4 a·way (-w)
1. *adv* From a particular thing or place: *ran away from the lion; sent the children away to boarding school*
    a. At or to a distance in space or time: *We live a block away from the park*
    b. At or by a considerable interval: *away back in the 17th century; away off on the horizon*

      a.   In a different direction; aside: *glanced away*

      b.   On the way: *We want to get away early in the day*

2.   In or into storage or safekeeping: *put the toys away; jewels locked away in a safe*

3.   Out of existence or notice: *The music faded away* Massacre of the Innocents

4.   So as to remove, separate, or eliminate: *chipped the paint away; cleared away the debris*

1.   From one's possession: *gave the tickets away* which have been commonly celebrated in the pagan cults before this and in which elements of Star and Nature worship can be traced;

2.   *Continuously; steadily: toiled away at the project for more than a year*

3.   *Freely; at will: Fire away!* the magnificent Orion, the mighty hunter *There are three stars in his belt which, as is well known, lie in a straight line pointing to Sirius They are not so bright as Sirius, but they are sufficiently bright to attract attention A long tradition gives them the name*
[1] Charles F Dupuis (Origine de Tous les Cultes, Paris, 1822)
was one of the earliest modern writers on these subjects

[4] *adj*

4.   Absent: *The neighbors are away* Mithra sets his mark on the forehead of his soldiers; he celebrates the oblation of bread;

5.   Distant, as in space or time: *The city is miles away The game was still a week away*

6.   Played on an opponent's field or grounds: *an away game*

7.   In golf, having the ball lying farthest from the hole and properly playing first among competitors

8.   *Baseball* Out: *bases loaded, with two away*

[Middle English, from Old English aweg : a-, *on*; see **a-**[1] + weg, *way*; see wegh- in Indo-European Roots]

Post
Silver
Age

Canto 70

Apollo 13 situation
Nixon launches incursion into Cambodia

students killed in shootings
Kent State and Jackson State Colleges

Jimi Hendrix and Janis Joplin die
cigarette advertising banned
EPA and National Air Quality Control Act

Vince Lombardi dies
Tom Dempsey kicks a record 63 yd field goal

And the human experience centers on i

As it opens the cityscape is black. A maroon sky with no visible sun. This is a panel of bleakness. There is little sign of control, no thinking, nothing weighing options ... once here you are the feral soul sleeping, the Shimbale in the heavens silent, binding soul to mortar, the sand to the cement. What once meant so much over there, tonight means heartache and pain; here -- this is the city, tonight this city is dark.

A shoulder turn follows most of what happens

There is an orange cat rumbling through a pizza box in a dumpster another resting on a riverside rusted lid. Bags of trash pyramid around ribbons of yesterdays newspapers. Odd how information fades in the rain. There is a bee struggling to swim to the side of a styrofoam food container. A worm huddled in a ball, naked, baking in the sun, ... inches from a puddle

lifts up his eyes to skies, and said, the hour is come; glorify life,
that life may also, within a circle glorify

eternal power over others life,
to many as life sent from afar
life on the earth enhanced:
yet there are too many commercials about trucks

And now in time, glorify your very self with the glory which before the world
I have manifested the name of justice to humanity

there they were, and you gave me time to help

We admire the hero of the sword

There is no problem big enough that violence cannot solve.

166

The man who uses his fist first looses the use of ideas

Now they have known that all things whatsoever you have given me are within
them   The one no blade can scar

For I have given to them the actions which they gave me
and they have seen them, received the freedoms availed
known surely

            that I came out for them and all they hold dear
            have believed that there is a better life awaiting

The ending is nothing more than a beginning.
A zeroed out balance. Inequities canceled
in the wake of sea against seashore.

This is all. Nothing wanting nothing.
It should seem
life would struggle for life

assist, render aid, help at all costs.

            This is not always the case.
this earth can be

paradise

this plane   one

But the hero is not a HUMAN he is alien to all around him.
And the deeds of many never suit the needs of one

For what is it to be human and not be flawed

            for the divinity

is all as mine are mine is thine
as are thine mine; and I am as divine
            in them as in them I

am no more in the world, but these are in the city, and I come to be.

Tonight I dwell on them:
I pray not for Metropolis,
but for them who live here
and have given me a home

What is it to be alive and have nothing to live for
The job of reporting the aftermath selling the many,
to afford suits and Italian shoes
            and if pushed too far
            meals that last all night

            every plate full

It is in the nature of things to fear pain. The fear of loss,
the knowledge of death, the hesitation to change ...

is never equal to the humdrum of joy.

in the aggregate this may function adequately
but on the individual is off center, off key,

all clocks stops, like old springs rust

It is very odd how difficult it seems
yet the matter itself presents no difficulty

to conceive of purity is error

I in them, and them in me, that they may be made perfect in one?
I have never tried to take from them this world,
or imagine that they should want removal from evil

This would undermine all that faults define

They are the city, even as I am of the city.
one must kill the gods they create

before the foundation of the world

I will come, be at the side of those whom have been given dearly
that they may be one, as are we.

epics of you,
epicenters on i

You hear stories of famous cats and hero dogs on suburban farms or english country lanes. But in the here, this city, not even rats eat well. The cycle knows how to leave it as you found it. Alone on the crisp evening after a light rain. This is a panel of bleakness.

Canto 71

Weather Underground bombs the Capitol
Mayday march
Louis Satchmo Armstrong and Door's Jim Morrison die
Bury My Heart at Wounded Knee published
school busing for racial desegregation ruled constitutional
Joe Frazier defends title against Muhammed Ali

The Ultimate

And fastened to a dying animal
It knows not what it is; and gather me
Into the artifice of eternity
Sailing to Byzantium; W.B. Yeats

The chain of death assembles in conception

in gloom

250,000 years ago
man on earth furies
an upright stance

While in space a scientist named Bertron
travels to a primeval Krypton to conduct
experiments under an adolescent red sun

This scientist worked without constraint
no morality or code of conduct to guide
his work to create the Ultimate form alive

a point above all, looking down making image to image
in a covered dome located in the unforgiving deserts
flaming sand storm days countered blue frozen nights

the surrounding was home to the prehistoric nature of tooth and bone,
a fitting place to begin, this man of science, sheltered from all but havoc

it was here he began to create.

excited by power the imagination floating across the ear and eye
Bertron carried with him, in stasis, an infant child stolen
from the civilization of Zantato from the planet Conte Ti

As all children from these peoples he was a light grey
wisps of white hair, bright red eyes, a tiny jagged smile

169

He played with Bertron's pointing finger

If all goes well my fine young friend, a crooked grin
you will do wondrous things, evil yes, but wondrous

In his arms like one would with favorite cat he threw the baby out
of the protective hatchway and into the pride of waiting creatures

The child began to cry, attracting dangers attention

At long last, they must have thought
approaching the child mouths wide open

and immediately the three axioms are fulfilled. Perception, form of an outward
generating spiral that will end, an upper limit, and regenerate into a new
perception/conception of poetic atmosphere, from high atop in a tower, a form following of
content, so to say, from a reborn voice, no matter its source.

The scientist waiting until danger passed
went out and gathered a tissue sample
from the remains and cloned another infant.

The process would be grown from whatever remained
a cycle of creation, life, destruction, reconstruction
in absurdity becoming tied to a dog's tail until the mind
can wrestle the abstract horrors

After ten years evolution began to stem
After twenty the baby was noticeably changed

thirty the thing could survive the environment
elude everything for days before being killed

If you love me let me know for Ultimately
the beginnings of the cycle are in the endings

Within the next century the remains of one tiny child
came looped with death would regenerate once killed

a learned response nurtured by nature
What killed it once will never kill again
Ultimate defense, or so said the proud

father becoming attached to the thing,
casually referring to it as the Ultimate

Transcending the confessional whine to universal statement of human condition.

as it hunted the creatures
that had killed it in the past
erased them all
into extinction.

The Ultimate lives to be alone

created a physical world and a realm of the spirit would meet, transform
one another, and interfuse one another with an energy. It was artifice,
the walls seemed to fold blending a cultural discourse of body and spirit.

decades of torture weighed on the seven foot tall thing
the mental anguish of what made it must be eradicated
and ultimately killed the scientist Bertron, grim and slow.

The Ultimate wandered the desert in irony
a fury for vicious murder yet nothing to slay

The Gyres ! the gyres ! Old Rocky Face, look forth;
Things thought too long can be no longer thought,
For beauty dies of beauty, worth of worth

Where there is an answer for death life intervenes

In the dead of night it caught sight of a flash
a starship landing near the destroyed dome
and began unloading supplies
not knowing Bertron was dead

The Ultimate boarded the ship unnoticed,
and now even the stars may tremble fear

for now a moment of doom has access to the stars.

Canto 72

Nixon visits China and Moscow
Senate passes SALT treaty and Equal Rights Amendment
J. Edgar Hoover dies
George Wallace shot
death penalty ruled unconstitutional
George McGovern accuses Nixon of Watergate break-in vows to remove US
presence in Vietnam
defeated by Nixon in Presidential bid
Life magazine folds
Roberto Clemente killed in air crash
Curt Flood's antitrust suit against baseball
Bob Seagren pole vaults 18'5 3/4"
Arab terrorists disrupt Olympics in Munich
Bobby Fisher defeats Boris Spassky.

Brainiac

Currently, Brainiac assumes control

even in light of poems razed

you from the material; dead, yet with Lazarus

in tow

We are all corpses, copies

lost data can be a devastating
kindred, tongue, people, nation

our spiritual estate of the rampaging monster Doomsday
for yet another attack against Superman and his allies.

is one of complete death, no life within at all.
Therefore no response. The sinful cannot change

Vril Dox or "Brainiac," held a coup, seizing control of the world's super computers

His mind can meld the binary relationships
of man and machine a freak show mentalist

We've Recovered over One Million Megabytes of Lost Data
But If you were here to help in the actions of others

it would seem that that the great ideals
from across the void, vast telepathic and psychokinetic powers

of the all that is American, fanatical promotions of truth and justice

As all wives say when I am of no use
their continued life alone concentrated on

my failures

When Brainiac began wasting away,
                where he forced to dream
                geneticists and cyberneticists
                to enhance his body.

Superman discovered Brainiac's rebirth too late,
and Brainiac retreated into space to further raid, quest

powers

As punishment, the atoms of his body were dispersed,
but his mind somehow managed to survive.

Where there is life there is hope; are all corpses,
Where death all things continue, copies of lost data

Canto 73

The Watergate scandal explodes (special prosecutors, 18 1/2 min. gap, Liddy, McCord, Dean, Erlichman, Grey, Richardson, Jaworski, Cox, Ervin, impeachment) Lyndon Johnson dies Vietnam peace accords signed occupation of Wounded Knee by Native American activists Vice President Spiro Agnew resigns Gerald Ford sworn in as Nixon resigns Roe vs. Wade abortion decision Chicago seven convicted American Graffiti OPEC oil embargo Alaska pipeline approved first athletic scholarship to a woman given to U. of Miami swimmer new Sears Tower tallest building in world O.J. Simpson sets NFL rushing record Billie Jean King beats Bobby Riggs

THE LEGION OF DOOM

Greatest Super-Villains Of All Time!

Superman speaks as the last survivor of the planet Earth
and tells of the incredible disaster unleashed by the Legion of Doom.

its times like these when no one seems to care
that pride in ones work comes at a price.
when all spectacle comes force upon blade
crank shaft over a slide rule, Intel over ADM

thirteen villains gathered together, the Hall of Doom
representing the ultimate arch-enemies; a foil of form

in order to destroy/ or /rule the world, the last will be first
and the thirteen will ride dark animators glory sky

when you first see
a horse it is frightening

a tiger swooping
a gentle cats sleep

but it is the man on top that call the eye upwards
to the sword or pistol on his side, a wool blanket

at the time of death what thoughts will swirl in my head
when energy departs for new horizons;
what thoughts will remain

              to challenge the combined strength of the Super Friends
                 Lex Luthor founded this Legion of Doom

          if one falls against many
          many against many

              on that day

          many will fall
          one will be won, held
          by the ones left standing

There is no telling what the evil mind can accomplish

      In a murky swamp
      Grodd the gorilla is frustrated
      by insipid plans for global conquest

Luthor silences him for Captain Cold
has recently been in contact with an advanced civilization
      from the planet of Venus

      The feminine yet ferocious Giganta is unimpressed
      but Bizarro calmly claims he can make it not work.

        Or rather 'to work'
        Luthor amends

Sinestro and Bizarro will fly to the Moon
  using an atomic laser they cut it in half
to retrieve the Robalt element deep within its core

        The astronauts of Moon Base One will be thrown into deep space
      and the debris will disrupt the solar flows and crash the Earth into the Sun

The Toyman will lure the Green Lantern to his planet of toys,
with well placed traps placing false distress calls

          sending the Super friends on a wild goose
        chase that will end them right out of the Universe

As The Legion of Doom
their ingenious plan goes into action

After repairing the NASA space station on the far side of the moon and
wishing its astronauts well

Hawkman, Green Lantern and The Dynamic Duo
in the Hawk Plane fly for home

They hear Superman's
distress call,
which is actually a Toyman
trick,
head off to find what
happened

Earth.

Frigid Captain Cold
sets out with his giant freezing ray, blue spun butter
freezing Washington D.C., San Francisco, New York.

Aquaman arrives to the scene of destruction
to find the sinister, humorous Riddler

[A question mark looms on the high seas]

only to be subdued by with the Noxium crystal. Luthor
and the others then plan their next target, Wonder Woman.

The cunning Cheetah tries to break into the Metropolis
Electrical Plant and fools Wonder Woman into harnessing a robot
rocket with her Magic Lasso.

We do not see her again

In Washington D.C the super intelligent android Brainiac

duplicates all of the world leaders,
replacing their forms with robotics

and their plan to conquest the Earth is almost set.

Black Manta and the hideous Scarecrow ends their plans
beaming the mental matter ray straight

through to all of the worlds peoples
through to all of the worlds television sets

They slip into the universe of Qward and leave behind three antimatter robots as a trap that
will destroy the Super Friends once they are touched.

Chief O'Hara informs them that Grodd and Solomon Grundy are
attempting to break into the Gotham City Treasury.

Superman and Black Vulcan
        race to intercept them.
Luthor's mind control paralyzes them.

        The Legion of Doom streak on their deadly course to worldwide conquest

                        …

A spaceship lands and three aliens emerge wondering what happened.

                The Earth in shambles,
                black crustings of life
                nothing moves in silence; no one is alive

                END OF WORLD NEAR - SUPER FRIENDS NO HELP!!

                no one is alive and nothing moves in silence

The aliens see the people of Earth never understood
that the use of force over force to solve problems
always brings not only chaos but ripples in space and time.

they decided it is in the universes best interest
to give the Earth life once more
a second chance at life and undo

                                and turn back time to before the disaster.
                                to relive their disasters
                                only with bit of help from new friends.

                The Legion of Doom
                tries to battle

rivals spin in orbits

                but are soon rounded up
                with the help of the mental matter ray.

The Legion of Doom
will never break away from justice or the Super Friends.

                        when you first see
                        a horse it is frightening

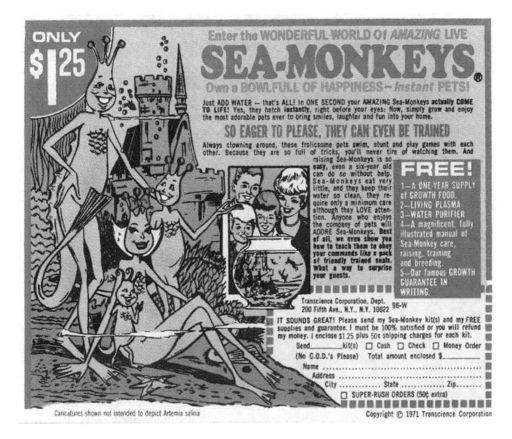

Canto 74

Earl Warren dies
amnesty proclamation for Vietnam draft resisters

Freedom of Information Act
Boston racial turmoil
                                    Deaths: Bud Abbott, Jack
Benny,
        Duke Ellington,
Cass Eliott, Charles Lindberg, Ed Sullivan
Patricia Hearst and SLO rob bank
        Henry Aaron passes Babe Ruths lifetime home run
        record
        Frank Robinson becomes first black manager in
        baseball

Little League baseball opens to girls

And there is always some man living on the outskirts of town
        looking for someone to blame for his misery, the hate keeps
        cold hearts warm when bathing in cold tap water.

Rusting orange site to site purging a set of objects, a situation,
        Between hatred and longing desire a chain of events
                which shall be the formula
                of that Particular emotion

And all laugh at him and throw Starbucks Coffee cups at him
        with this the poet feels and hopes to evoke in the pedestrian
        that sense of the unshaven wrinkled oxford shirt eating

                mac and strung cheese
                in chains truly described
                was drawn in as if under a spell

Although the cosmos stills laughs
this is potentially the strongest being in existence

Canto 75

military academies admit women
Woman attempts to assassinate President Ford, twice,
Supreme Court bans forced confinement of mental patients

Jimmy Hoffa disappearance
Thorton Wilder dies
        school bussing for racial balance begins
voluntary change to metric system in ten years planned
Hearst captured

Doomsday

Mere anarchy is loosed upon the world,
The blood-dimmed tide is loosed, and everywhere
The ceremony of innocence is drowned;
        The Second Coming; W.B. Yeats

Later, the Ultimate made his way to the far side of the galaxy
the ravaged stolen spaceship flew a path, a progression of time,
a circle when looking down upon it, a gyre, a world history

was eventually caught in the orbit of the planet Khundia, the inhabitants,
an advanced feudal civilization whose people demanded action hand in hand
with honor : Thus the end of our cycle will come amidst a combat ceremony

The dominant houses of Ebon and Krimsn did battle
Flags unfurled in the blues, golds and red circles
representing the moons and her thirty-seven phases

The wish to stay alive comes in short bursts and when the leader of the house of Ebon
saw the rocket hit over the mountain tops, Now, is already in the period of pure anarchy
This is the day of our doom. And so the Ultimate ravaged to become known as

The new and full moon are the periods where time begins end over ends

growth between evolution of the human soul over time
a thousand years a single civilization a prevailing myth

However, it is not an end in the right sense of the word, arise of new

Doomsday made its way across Khundia meeting valiant attacks and challenges
all doomed to failure, smashed with bone and hopes there was never anything left

180

here relation to death is a matter of business, the corruption and pollution of honor constituting an obstacle to action, a crime against its own purpose

The leader of the house of Ebon, Kobald, saw the Doomsday fall from the sky if it came to this planet it can leave and so devised a method to send it off world in a rocket. Kobald would engage the creature and bait it to the rocket, but how?

to survive for those brief minutes before the rocket could launch both off world into orbit he would have to survive long enough

but existence is not enough he would need a shield like the ones of heroes of old times told over camp fires

The framework of his own mythology becomes a new device.

the Khundian scientists create a genuine armor bonded with an invigorating spirit moving closer towards his own identity. This may work if …

When Doomsday saw the shining thing it ran after it hit it with a left hand sending it flying into an iron shell

of the rocket. Kobald's plan had worked he and Doomsday wrestled while rocketing into outer space.

One giant leap for the planet Khundia

"It is through our combined efforts that this our greatest tragedy is merged with our greatest triumph. We have conquered the boundaries of gravity

and removed the very threat to our survival – a common enemy has made common friends – together we will enter the heavens and look on the face of gods – remember this day, it mirrors a still sky"

The rocket exploded killing Kobald and the monster was sent hurtling

lost through space in the remains of the rocket ship

Canto 76

The U.S. Bicentennial
Alex Haley's Roots published

Jimmy Carter defeats Ford for presidency
transsexual Renee Richards barred from US Open tennis
Concorde initiates first supersonic commercial flight

Detroit stops building convertibles
Red Dye No. 2 banned

The Day of Doom

**Michael Wigglesworth,
first published in1662**
[selections 1 – 18 of 225]

Still was the night, serene and bright,
    when all men sleeping lay:
Calm was the season, and carnal reason
    thought so 'twould last of ay.
Soul take thine ease, let sorrow cease,
    much good thou hast in store:
this was their song, their cups among,
    the evening before.

Wallowing in all kind of sin,
    vile wretches lay secure:
The best of men had scarcely then
    their lamps kept in good ure.
Virgins unwise, who though disguise
    among the best were numbered,
Had closed their eyes: yea and the wise
    through sloth and frailty slumbered.

Like as of old, when men grow bold
    God's threat'nings to contemn,
Who stopped their ear, and would not hear,
    when Mercy warned them:
But took their course, without remorse,
    till God began to pour
Destruction the world upon
    in a tempestuous shower.

They put away the evil day,
    and drowned their care and fears,
Till drowned were they, and swept away
    by vengeance unawares:

So at the last, whilst men sleep fast
        in their security,
Surprised they are in such a snare
        as cometh suddenly.

For at midnight brake forth a light,
        which turned the night to day,
And speedily an hideous cry
        did all the world dismay
Sinners awake, their hearts do ache
        trembling their loins surpriseth;
Amazed with fear, by what they can hear,
        each one of them ariseth.

They rush from beds with giddy heads,
        and to their windows run,
Viewing this light, which shines more bright
        then doth the noon-day sun.
Straightway appears (they see't with tears)
        the Son of God most dread;
Who with His train comes on amain
        to judge both quick and dead.

Before his face the Heav'ns gave place,
        and skies are rent asunder,
With mighty voice, and hideous noise,
        more terrible than thunder
His brightness damps Heav'ns glorious lamp
        and makes them hide their heads,
As if afraid and quite dismayed,
        they quit their wonted steads.

Ye sons of men that durst condems
        the threat'ning of God's word,
How cheer you now? your hearts, I trow,
        are thrilled as with the sword,
Now atheist blind, whose brutish mind
        a God could never see,
Dost thou perceive, dost now believe,
        that Christ thy Judge shall be?

Stout courages, (whose hardiness
        could death and hell out-face)
Are you as bold now you behold
        your Judge draw near apace?
They cry, no, no: alas! and woe!
        our courage all is gone:
Our hardiness (fool hardiness)
        hath us undone, undone.

No heart so bold but now grows cold
        and almost dead with fear:
No eye so dry, but now can cry,
        and pour out many a tear.

Earth's potentates and powerful states,
   captains and men of might
Are quite abashed, their courage dashed
   at this most dreadful sight

Mean men lament, great men do rent
   their robes, and tear their hair;
They do not spare their flesh to tear
   through terrible despair.
All kindreds wail: all hearts do fail:
   horror the worlds doth fill
With weeping eyes, and loud out-cries,
   yet knows not how to kill.

Some hide themselves in caves and delves,
   in places under ground:
Some rashly leap in to the deep,
   to scape by being drowned:
Some to the rocks (Oh senseless blocks!)
   and woody mountains run,
That there they might this fearful sight,
   and dreaded presence shun.

In vain do they to mountains say,
   "Fall on us and us hide
From Judge's ire, more hot than fire,
   from who might it abide?"
No hiding place ca from His face,
   sinners at all conceal,
Whose flaming yes hid things doth 'spy,
   and darkest things reveal

The Judge draws nigh, exalted high
   upon a lofty throne,
Amidst the throng of angels strong,
   ol, Israel's Holy One!
The excellence of Whose presence
   and awful Majesty,
Amazeth Nature, and every creature,
   doth more than terrify.

The mountains smoke, the hills are shook,
   The earth is rent and torn,
As if she should be clean dissolved,
   or from the center born,
The sea doth roar, forsakes the shore
   and shrinks away for fear;
The wild beasts flee to the sea,
   so soon as He draws near.

Whose glory bright, whose wondrous might,
   whose power imperial,

So far surpass whatever was
in realms terrestrial;
That tongues of men (now Angel's pen)
cannot the same express
And therefore I must pass it by,
lest speaking should transgress.

Before His throne a trump is blown,
proclaiming the Day Of Doom:
Forthwith He cries, "*Ye dead arise,
and unto Judgment come.*"
No sooner said, but 'tis obeyed;
sepulchers opened are:
Dead bodies all rise to His call,
and's mighty power declare.

Both sea and land, at His command,
their dead at once surrender:
The fire and air constrained are
also their dead to tender.
The mighty word of the great Lord
links body and soul together
Both of the just, and the unjust,
to part no more forever.

Canto 77

President Carter pardons Vietnam draft resisters
neutron bomb developed
Werner von Braun dies
      Star Wars released
Groucho Marx and the King: Elvis Presley die
Roots miniseries televised
Space Shuttle Enterprise makes 1st free flight
Courageous wins America's Cup

Doomsday Returns

A shape with lion body and the head of a man,
A gaze blank and pitiless as the sun,
Is moving its slow thighs, while all about it
Reel shadows of the indignant desert birds.
The darkness drops again; but now I know

The Second Coming; W.B. Yeats

After a century of traveling across space Doomsday fell from the heavens
and again crashed into a field on the planet Calaton, a world of gardens,
mountain streams, fruits and honey; many would consider this the ultimate

    civilization of humanoids who want for nothing, the needs of the many met
by the workers and artists of the world: social order with little or no suffering

        These peoples were ruled by a family line chosen
for their DNA, a strain giving metahuman powers

    It was the strength and actions of these Meta
that deemed their place in the congress

    And when a common evil emerges uncommon valor prevails
many met the unspoken challenge of Doomsday
many died with little effort exerted against them.

        Three years of ruthless attacks took a heavy toll
The Floating Gardens of Zentax has fallen, the green
pastures of Ellison run bloody red, and the Ice Castle
way waste in glimmering shards

    only the only area that stood was the capital city of Mantela

If one Meta, or three could not defeat this creature then what if all
harnessed as one would be strong enough to stop this beast, or so

the royal scientists devised. and in time all members congressed

their metahuman life forces were drained and channeled
into a containment a whole composed of a number of different parts

The Radiant,
a being of pure energy,
was born.

It is known that Doomsday can be killed. However,
when killed he will revive, return from deaths grasp
evolved to a beyond that strength which killed him

The battle between Doomsday and the Radiant lasted over a week.

The horror in these events use, as their dominant theme and symbol, the day of doom
a quarrel unable to make good a defense
so we shall chant over to ourselves and listen
to the reasons that we have given as a countercharm to her spell

. . . for we have come to see that we must not take
such death seriously as a serious thing that lays hold
on truth, but that he who lends an ear to it must be on guard
fearing for the polity in his soul

belongs to the order of compounds
in the same way as all other things
which form a single whole,

must be on his guard the going back beyond the polity of the soul to the polis.

The whole belongs to the forming of many under the umbrella of a one entity. Does this
match the idea of the soul. I am not qualified to assert any one way or an other.

this I am sure was part of his secret ability, after becoming unquestionably the master, to
remain always a contemporary

The Radiant finally prevailed in a final blast of energy
that laid waste to a fifth of Calaton, destroying itself
in the process.

The body of Doomsday fell, motionless

The Radiant dissipated

to prevent its Doomsday from escaping in an afterlife
the people gathered up the body of the creature,

cloaked it
chained it

and was sent into the void
where it drifts for 245,000 years

That twenty centuries of stony sleep
Were vexed to nightmare by a rocking cradle,

And what rough beast, its hour come round at last,
Slouches towards Bethlehem to be born?

The Second Coming; W.B. Yeats

Canto 78

Love Canal pronounced a disaster area
Jim Jones and followers die in Guyana
Mayor of San Francisco shot to death
Norman Rockwell dies
Leon Spinks defeats Muhammed Ali
Pete Rose youngest player to get 3000 career hits

SUPERMAN: A MOVIE

FADE IN:

EXT. METROPOLIS - AERIAL - NIGHT

ROLL CREDITS:

JOHN WILLIAMS THEME BEGINS:

Snow swirls around the tall buildings of downtown Metropolis.

EXT. EXCELSIOR HOTEL - NIGHT

Cars, taxis, limos line the street. A cab pulls up and MAN
in tuxedo moves into:

INT. EXCELSIOR HOTEL - BALLROOM - NIGHT

THROUGH arriving guests we PICK UP a man climbing a grand
staircase to the ballroom.

ANGLE - MAIN LOBBY

The man hands his coat to bell boy and thanks him with a handshake.
When he turns we get our first view of MR. CLARK KENT, a tall,
wholesome, well dressed man, clean shaven dark glasses.

He moves from the outer lobby into an elaborately decorated
ballroom, a fundraiser dinner is taking place. Doctors, lawyers,
politicians, reporters and their spouses mingle. Women sit near the
buffet, men talk by the bar. The room is packed.

A banner over the podium says: "METROPOLIS ARTS FOUNDATION"

KENT is handed a glass of champagne, which he promptly sets on
another waiter's passing tray.

JOHNSON (V.O.)

CLARK...

MR. JOHNSON, a portly politician, pulls KENT over to a group
of lawyers & politician gathered around a bar smoking cigars.

JOHNSON

So Kent what are you doing here? The Planet not saving the world
this week?

KENT
No, we get a night off every now and again. How do you find the
exhibits?

SENETOR KENNEY
What are you drinking MR.KENT? No, strings attached, I promise.

KENT
On the house, huh?
(to bartender)
Tonic water with lime.

Everyone smiles.

KENT
Never get me to sell my soul for only one drink ...

His tone silences the group. KENT takes his drink.

KENT
(to Kenny)
... But if you get any more Capitals tickets, give me a call.

The group laughs, KENT extracts himself and CREDITS CONTINUE OVER -

CUT TO:

KENT

Moving through the crowd.

CUT TO:

KENT

Nearly gets run over in the follow-through of a swing dancer.

KENT
You're not sliding right, Eric. Don't lead with your hip.

He keeps moving.

SWING MAN
Thanks, CLARK...

CUT TO:

ANGLE - ABOVE

JIMMY OLSEN, totally out of her element amid the formal classiness
surrounding him. He is varsity sweater over white T-shirt and stares
at an art exhibit in utter confusion.

OLSEN
(dripping sarcasm)
I'm so glad you talked me into coming, CLARK ... What do you think
that is?

CLARK
It's the "Mythological Landscape" by Milan Kunc it says that there
is something wrong. The hero is laying on the grass and dreaming. On
the bottom an image of a toadstool arises from the ground. Then the
space opens over the dreaming hero and this is what he sees. Two
black swans upon a shimmering red lake. Only a constricted strip of
green separates the water surface from an illuminated red sky filled
with stars. A castle off in the distance, and a unicorn with a naked
woman playing a flute. the sexual element is quite obvious, she
rides against the red sky. So the hero dreaming of sex with eyes
wide open forgets about the order of things and looses the world.

OLSEN
Right, speaking of which you said Suzy from the copy room was
coming, but you didn't say with Jordan from Accounting

CLARK
Cheer up Jimmy. This night has a good cause ... We bought 100
tickets and needed someone to use them. Besides you need to get out
of the dark room more.

He smiles. He moves on.

ANGLE - PARTY

KENT continues down the bar when he spots a friend...

KENT
Hey, Henry.

MR. HENRY MILLER turns, smiles. Mid-40s, head of the University
Space Research Center.

MILLER
CLARK, I just saw someone who wanted to meet you...

Just then KENT spots an attractive WOMAN, late thirties, wearing a
sophisticated, simple black gown. She's surrounded by a group of men
hanging on her every word. She and KENT catch a look and hold it.

MILLER (V.O.)
CLARK KENT... Derrick Teufel. Derrick is working on the KTON-10
trials for Lexcorp.

KENT turns to meet MR. DERRICK TEUFEL, late 30s, tan, smiling.
Teufel extends his hand...

TEUFEL
MR. KENT... Sorry, we've been trading phone calls last few days ...
something about a radiation report you wanted more information on?

KENT
(suddenly attentive)
Yeah... There were a few anomalies found in a NASA meteorite report
and I was hoping you might be . . .

TEUFEL
I'll be in my office in the morning and we can give it a good look.
Is that a good time for you?

KENT
Sure.

TEUFEL
(holds KENT'S look, then to Miller)
See you, Henry.

Teufel moves on. KENT watches him move towards the buffet table,
then changes attention on the Woman he just saw. She's gone. He and
Miller move together through the party.

They reach the Woman in black gown, his wife, LOIS LANE. KENT
kisses her passionately.

MILLER
You look fabulous, Lois.

He kisses Lois.

LOIS (WOMAN)
Hello, Henry.

MILLER
(to KENT)
We'll have lunch tomorrow at one.

Miller leaves. KENT looks at his wife.

KENT
(Whispers in her ear)
I've found something, we should leave.

LOIS
Wouldn't that be unexpected?

CUT TO: (MOMENTS LATER)

LOIS
(to her friends)
I'm sorry, I have to get my husband home.

They say their good-byes and pass Miller's table. Miller shakes
Clark's hand in passing. From across the room we see Teufel
watching.

INT. KENT'S SEDAN - NIGHT

KENT and Lois driving home. She runs her fingers through his hair as
he drives.

KENT
Lois, I will always loved you.

CUT TO: (LATER THAT NIGHT)

SUPERMAN flies overhead of LEXCORP with his X-Ray vision and his
Super hearing Superman listens in overhead.

Atom Man is standing on a platform giving a thank you speech to the
workers of the LEXCORP. The hard work that they brought to bear, had
stolen the Kryptonite, used the meteor to transform Henry Miller
into The Atom Man. With Kryptonite streaming through his veins he
would be the perfect opponent to Superman. The Kryptonite would
drain his powers so any human would be able to defeat him in regular
combat.

Atom Man moves to the last of his speech as SUPERMAN enters at the
flies through a window.

ATOM MAN
... And I especially would like to thank my researchers, Teufel
(whose name means "The Devil" in German) to helped me ...

Atom Man stops his speech - stunned to see SUPERMAN.

ATOM MAN
SUPERMAN ...

SUPERMAN
What's wrong, Henry? Surprised?

SUPERMAN begins moving down the aisle past the tables of scientists
toward the podium.

Stunned expressions.

SUPERMAN continues to the front, talking to Atom Man as if the room
were empty.

SUPERMAN
After Teufel died, you were the only one that had access to the
reports.

Atom Man remains calm.

ATOM MAN
Reports? What are you?

SUPERMAN
You switched the samples and falsified the reports so you could
tamper with the Kryptonite, and form yourself into this.

ATOM MAN
Superman, I don't know what you're talking about?...

192

Atom Man stares at SUPERMAN and for the first time we see a flicker of concern.

SUPERMAN
You almost pulled it off, Henry. But I know all about it now, and I can prove it.

Atom Man and SUPERMAN hold a look. Atom Man turns

ATOM MAN
Superman, if you want to talk -

SUPERMAN
I didn't come here to talk

Atom Man moves toward an exit.

ON ATOM MAN

Moves through a door and exits into...

HALLWAY

SUPERMAN follows moving forward to reach the door.

CUT TO:

EXT. HELICOPTER - NIGHT

ROARING over Metropolis skyline. The bright red sign of Dada Cola looms ahead.

CUT TO:

INT. HALLWAY

Atom Man moves down hallway and turns into a laboratory. A moment later SUPERMAN follow and enters the...

LABORATORY

... and is immediately smashed with a chair by Atom Man.
SUPERMAN goes flying, stunned. Atom Man locks the door.

ATOM MAN
Your best quality, Superman, is that you don't give up -

Atom Man pulls SUPERMAN to his feet.

ATOM MAN
... even when it's clearly in your best interest to...

He hits him again, drives him back.

SUPERMAN tries to recover as Atom Man relentlessly stays on him. He pulls him up, slams him against the fire escape doors.

ATOM MAN
I always knew that I'd have to kill you.

He drives a blow into SUPERMAN'S stomach.

ATOM MAN
Now, I must thank you for giving me the pleasure tonight

He shoves SUPERMAN through the door out into...

EXT. FIRE ESCAPE BALCONY - NIGHT

... and almost over the railing. SUPERMAN grabs the rail to keep
from dropping to the street. Atom Man closes on him, but SUPERMAN
rolls away at the last minute and knocks Atom Man back against the
other side of fire escape.

SUPERMAN
You missed your chance, Henry...

Atom Man charges SUPERMAN, but SUPERMAN drives him back with two
crushing blows that send Atom Man down the stairs.

SUPERMAN moves down the stairs after him - passing under a security
camera.

CUT TO:

INT. SECURITY ROOM - NIGHT

A room lined with security monitors. Two security guards sit in
front of their console.

On screen: We see SUPERMAN moving down the stairs toward Atom Man,
who pulls himself to his feet.

EXT. ROOFTOP FIRE ESCAPE - NIGHT

Atom Man rises to his feet, swings, but SUPERMAN blocks the blow and
lands another that sends Atom Man down another set of stairs to the
roof.

SUPERMAN
You would sell out your country, would use Kryptonite to weaken me?
Well how weakened am I now?

SUPERMAN pulls Atom Man to his feet. They are silhouetted by the
lights of the city skyline.

SUPERMAN
I want to know, Henry... was it worth it...?

ATOM MAN
This thing is bigger than even you think, Superman. You can't stop
it.

He hits Atom Man again with tremendous force, knocking him against
the guard rail. Atom Man stares over the edge - the street appears
far below.

SUPERMAN reaches Atom Man and draws to hit him again as the
HELICOPTER suddenly ROARS over the rooftop. Its beam hits the two
men and a VOICE booms from the helicopter:

194

VOICE FROM HELICOPTER (V.O.)
Metropolis police. Freeze.

In the instant of shock, Atom Man knees SUPERMAN and bolts.

INT. SECURITY - NIGHT

the security monitors catch SUPERMAN and Atom Man.

EXT. ROOF - NIGHT

Atom Man runs.

SUPERMAN recovers, sees Atom Man moving down a fire escape toward
him, and Atom Man escaping. He goes after Atom Man.

The helicopter circles back over the roof, illuminating the rooftop.

HELICOPTER PILOT (V.O.)
I've got a visual on SUPERMAN. He's in pursuit.

The helicopter swings out to keep SUPERMAN in sight.

ANGLE - ATOM MAN

SUPERMAN follows.

The helicopter circles and follows from above.

FOLLOWING SUPERMAN. Its beam tracking SUPERMAN across the rooftop.
SUPERMAN is gaining ground on Atom Man. Charges toward - SUPERMAN
slams Atom Man hard.

Atom Man's head rocks from the impact.

Atom Man struggles but SUPERMAN has him in control. Slams him down
hard again.

HELICOPTER

Circles, illuminates the struggle in its spotlight

SUPERMAN slams Atom Man one more time against the wall and the
supports give way, sending SUPERMAN and Atom Man into an elevator
shaft

INT. ELEVATOR SHAFT - NIGHT

SUPERMAN and Atom Man, locked together, fall down the shaft and
crash onto the roof of the descending elevator car. Atom Man crashes
through the ceiling into the car. SUPERMAN hits and slides across
the roof to the edge, stopping himself, just before he falls into
the shaft. An
elevator car rushes toward him out of the blackness.

SUPERMAN'S car disappears into the darkness.

CUT TO:

INT. ELEVATOR CAR - NIGHT

Atom Man pulls himself to his feet. Hits the emergency stop and the doors open. He disappears into...

HALLWAY - NIGHT

INT. ELEVATOR CAR

SUPERMAN drops from the ceiling into the car and moves carefully into the hallway.

... Dimly lit, filled with NOISY MACHINERY.

Atom Man pushes through the darkness toward an exit, tries the door. It is locked. He keeps moving.

SUPERMAN

Follows Atom Man's trail. He stops to get his bearings, sees shadow at the far end of the room. SUPERMAN closes in. He sees a shadow again, turns the corner and is about to hit it he realizes it's not Atom Man, but a terrified worker.

SUPERMAN moves away from the terrified man, when he hears a voice from the other end of the room.

ON ATOM MAN

Moving behind machinery, sees light at far end of the room

CUT TO:

SUPERMAN

Moves instinctively back into the machinery and carts near a conveyor belt.

SUPERMAN

Waits considering his next move.

ATOM MAN

Also waiting realizes this is his last battle. He moves behind the steps into an open path. From here he can see straight back to the hallway.

ATOM MAN

Steps out of the shadows, Atom Man moves toward Superman with a gun.

SUPERMAN

He knows Atom Man is armed with his Kryptonite ray.

ATOM MAN

Steps INTO FRAME behind him and slowly takes aim. Just before he fires however he hears...

SUPERMAN (O.S.)
Hey, Henry ...

Atom Man turns toward the voice as SUPERMAN swings a stick and
clobbers him - sending the gun spinning on the floor and under a
machine.

SUPERMAN, exhausted, leans against the wall.

They hold a look as deputies and police flood into the room
surrounding SUPERMAN and handcuff Atom Man.

CUT TO
EXT. - NIGHT (LATER)

Metropolis Police hold back crowds of onlookers. Police cars and
vans, television news trucks struggle for space to be the first to
interview the Man of Steel.

Atom Man, on a stretcher, loaded into an ambulance. The doors close.

REPORTERS and television cameramen line the sidewalk giving reports
and interviewing any who saw the excitement.

CUT TO:

INT. LEXCORP - NIGHT

SUPERMAN is escorted out into the waiting chaos. There he sees Lois
Lane, Their eyes meet in all of the ruckus. Reporters crowd forward,
yelling questions.

REPORTER
SUPERMAN, is it true you can almost lost all of your powers to Atom
Man!

LOIS LANE
(to police)
Get them back.

SUPERMAN pauses, then grabs Lois in his arms and kisses her twirling
above the sidewalk. This is the image that will be on all of the
morning newspapers.

As we PULL UP we see SUPERMAN'S embrace - at first they are alone on
the avenue - then gradually PAN joined by other passing people until
finally becoming integrated in the movements, jumble and lights of
the city.

FADE OUT

THE END

Canto 79

Iran takes American hostages
>> federal bailout of Chrysler
the Duke
>> John Wayne
>> dies

Three Mile Island nuclear accident
Department of Education formed

Our Polis

> Our polis, it turns out here, is the very whole world,
> the State, The System, the totality that it is incumbent
> on writers to "invert" and oppose "by discovering the
> totality of any – every -- single one of us."
>
> *The Methodology is the Form, Charles* Olson

Confucius says, brings one to the goal: nothing is possible without doing it
Then enter the city, our polis as a creature of nature following the code
and those other creations of nature may stay outside with the trees

If this all or nothing tactic, this mastery of craft, this totalitarian deconstruction,
this cleansing of mud puddles this production of wooden legal documents

than anything anyone says who holds a long dedicated apprenticeship to poetry;
the poem can bite his thumb to all … as does the anarchist to the prince of cats.
Can poetry matter in a world of color televisions sets and franchise gloss?

Never look back, they may be gaining on you; to remain always a contemporary
this I am sure was part of his secret ability, after becoming the master, decisively

This is the poem and its destruction is developed within its pages, can Superman matter
when there is nothing for him to chase, or the chase not brought to him, come where is the
carry over, the mental *can do* that we rely on every Saturday morning

The mind body connection is found in what we purchase, the gift of memory
to hold in the hand that purple wave washing months of pain, to never forget

The end of poetry is outside, on the hill, entrenched, waiting to battle the winds
Superman cultivated a republic in The City of God, that unrealities, fantasies,
mere ideas, can never be destroyed. Superman understood this clearly.

Metropolis belongs to its people, that sum of parts working in concert, walking the streets, a ballet in different rhythms, avant contemporary

The occasions developed folklore and supernatural legend. Often beautiful renditions
a beautiful strong woman, a wandering hero, rarefied souls. As in the music of Mozart,
a cry for release from circumstance is present, his unfulfilled love for Lois Lane.

Sometimes the hero must die for the city to continue, to use the bomb so carefully
dusted, polished to pleasure oneself or to keep in practice, to drill

in The City of God that unreality is found
in what we purchase
a descript cry for release;

then enter the city, our polis as a creature of nature;
nothing is possible without doing it Become the drill,

circumstance is present, cultivate a republic, as in the music of Mozart

visualize salvation from your armchair -- can poetry matter in a world of color

Pre
Modern
Age

Canto 80

aborted Iranian hostage rescue mission
US hockey team wins gold in winter Olympics
          Abscam
Soviets invade Afghanistan
eruption of Mt. St. Helens
          Mae West dies

Ronald Reagan elected president
Ford Motors loses Pinto case
          Who Shot J.R. episode on Dallas
          John Lennon shot and killed

US boycotts Moscow summer Olympics
Jesse Owens dies

When Plato calls on the listener he chooses to hold our hand
then the material of verse will shift under the notion of a Republic
Lois it's 9:50 PM and I am going to be late again it seems
The whole belongs to the forming of many under the umbrella
through this insight is a clear example to demonstrate the master
as the keystone in a roman arch, a dreamer visionary former king
Sing in their high and lonely melody, a greek chorus echoing
contained, condensed, compressed; reappearing earthly images

surrounding the real and the myth of old, here we have a Superman
bound by the drawing near for songs to hear the strange things said
You'll never get out of this maze, bright hearts of those long dead
back beyond the Polis, the polites, the citizen brings to the whole
don't keep my dinner warm, this ethereal high and lonely melody
the poet is blinded by eternal beauty only to have it wander away

Canto 81

Iranian hostage crisis ends
as President Reagan assumes office
Reagan shot
Reagan fires air traffic controlers on strike

first women Supreme Court Justice Sandra Day O'Conner
two Libyan jets shot down
IBM introduces the PC
MTV

Cholesterol linked to heart disease
Joe Louis dies.

the poet is blinded by eternal beauty only to have it wander away
When Plato calls on the listener he chooses to hold our hand
into the world: again, I leave this ethereal high and lonely melody
then the material of verse will shift under the notion of a Republic
as the keystone in a roman arch, a dreamer visionary former king
contained, condensed, compressed; reappearing earthly images
back beyond the Polis, the polites, the citizen bring to the whole

Sing in their high and lonely melody, a greek chorus echoing
bound by the drawing near for songs to hear the strange things said
Lois it's 9:50 PM and I am going to be late again it seems
but I will see you again, and your heart shall rejoice, bright hearts
of those long dead surrounding the real and the myth of old
through this insight is a clear example to demonstrate the master

Canto 82

recession peaks with falling unemployment and cost of living
Reagan proposes MX missile
US Marines land in Beirut
                    Air Florida jet crashes into a bridge in
                    Washington DC
                    first space shuttle flight
Ayn Rand dies
seven die from cyanide laced Tylenol capsules

Alexander Haig resigns
first artificial heart

You'll never get out of this maze, bright hearts of those long dead
as the keystone in a roman arch, their metahuman life forces
were drained and channeled into a containment vessel.

the poet is blinded by eternal beauty only to have it wander away

through this insight is a clear example to demonstrate the master
a being of pure energy, this ethereal high and lonely melody
then the material of verse will shift under the notion of a Republic

back beyond the Polis, the polites, the citizen bring to the whole

When Plato calls on the listener he chooses to hold our hand
                                    reappearing earthly images

surrounding the real and the myth of old, he will guide you
into all truth whosoever kills you will think he does God service.

Canto 83

Car bomb destroys US embassy in Beirut
Cabbage Patch Doll

USSR downs South Korean Airliner
US invasion of Grenada

video tape players
final episode of M*A*S*H

Sally Ride first woman and Guion Bluford first black in space
holiday named for Martin Luther King Jr.

the word might be fulfilled that is written in their law,
         They hated me without a cause from the beginning

bound by the drawing near for songs to hear the strange things said
         back beyond the Polis, the polites, the citizen can bring the whole

         then the material of verse will shift under the Republic of the real
         Lois it's 9:50 PM and I am going to be late again it seems

The whole belongs to the forming of many under open raining skies
         through this example

the poet is blind in the face of beauty only to have it wander away
         as the keystone in a roman arch, a dreamer visionary former king

surrounding the real and the myth of old, here we have a Superman
         contained, condensed, compressed; reappearing earthly images

         don't keep my dinner warm, this ethereal high and lonely melody
         Sing in their high and lonely melody, a greek chorus echoing

Canto 84

first planet detected outside this solar system
After 117 years US resumes diplomatic relations with the
Vatican

       LA Olympics without presence of the Eastern Block in
          retaliation for Carter's Olympics boycott in 80
            AIDS virus identified
              chicken pox vaccine developed
    Reagan reelected
    Donald Duck turns 50
           Ansel Adams and Count Basie
die
US Marines withdraw from Lebanon
runner Jim Fixx dies running

the listener prefers to hold hands
the material of verse will wear it seems

through this insight
is a clear example of the keystone

echoing
reappearing earthly images

the real
bound by the drawing
this maze

of bright hearts
back beyond the Polis,
the whole

the poet wanders away
blind by beauty

Canto 85

sanctions on South Africa for
apartheid
Achille Lauro high jacked in the
Mediterranean

Rock Hudson dies of AIDS
US dollar devalued
leaded gasoline banned

McAuliffe first teacher chosen for space shuttle mission
New Coke disaster and reversion to Coca-Cola classic

Roger Maris dies
Nolan fans his 4000th batter

These things I command you, that ye love one another
then the material of the republic will shift under this notion

of greater love

hath no man any greater than this, that
a man lay down his life for his friends

this the keystone in the arch, love one another, as I have loved you

surround the real and the myth of old,
bound by the drawing near for songs
to hear the strange things said

this maze that ye bear much fruit

don't keep my dinner warm,
Lois I love you and miss you

and my words abide in you
and they are burned, cast forth as a branch,
and is withered beauty wandering away

Modern Age

Canto 86

Space Shuttle Challenger disaster
US air strikes against Libya
      International Court of Justice rules US actions
against Nicaragua are illegal
      Iran-Contra affair exposed

Cary Grant dies
      Ivan Boesky brought down in Wall Street
scandal
      Benny Goodman and Rudy Vallee die

Hand Across America
genetic engineered organisms
Congress names the rose the official US flower

wandering

      while you read try to keep up

the cause unstoppable

    a fighter for all things well fought
      Even the evil Lex Luthor
      all attempts, plans, deceits

never,

      with all things human
      at his whim, command
      able to completely stop

      the Man of Tomorrow

But tonight there is blended treachery

Metropolis University

There is an elderly security guard walking down the darkened hallways
of the university

Hand on a flashlight, keys jingling to frighten off ghosts or other hidden things

Its almost too good to be true.
The first in a series of things
abruptly out of place is the chair

floating in mid air, a green man grinning and the old man drops his keys, flashlight

fumbles for his radio but that too in fright, drops to the ground. The mans knees knock

Take me to the laboratory database
I will take you to the database

You will search through the computers, do you know computers
I know computers, I will search for you

Good little man and if you are a good little man I will let you forget
good little man   forget

Begin search: Doomsday
Doomsday, processing

under covers with a flashlight

Topping tonight's Eyewitness News

There are no late game miracles

There are conjunctions between
what entertains at 6 & 11 and
what ghastliness gets shown

shooting of a child entering school
a drunk driver, the impending war
        politicians dance in a ring

that tropical storm moving northwest
buckeye broncos neither won or lost
there are no late game miracles here

The goal here is to report on what we can bear,
not explain our universe as philosophy, as pulp

do nothing about it … another will have this slot soon,
buy what is advertised, off you go, bed at eleven thirty

The news is never what it could be

        Taught simulate speaking
        entertaining & enchanting

This as is in all things determined by sales and consumer demand

When we enter the pages of Superman, this ring of a bell
clouds of the real slip through fingers, burning 4 color inks
hiding in a setting where the villain, the one responsible
is caught in full view of the city, no need for lengthy trials,

he plead guilty to Superman
in his hideout crawling in tears,
        for being caught
        for losing the prize

The greatest foe will always be your own potential

        Taught simulate speaking
        entertaining & enchanting

This as is in all things determined by sales and consumer demand

Brainiac back at the lair

A rust colored cave in the middle 2 miles below
the Earths crust a large computer blinks rapidly

Brainiac's mind somehow manages to survive nestled within the electrical fibers

> Where there is life there is hope; are all corpses,
> Where death all things continue, copies of lost data

while wandering the galaxy as a spray of restless atoms bound by mental energy alone
Hatred, anger, seething revenge, loathing the life that is Superman, he must pay for this
and that this is powerful hatred, and powerful hate can make, contribute forward marvels

> he finds an ancient space ship long since abandoned
> > Brainiac takes hold and clings to the
> > negative of the ships main computers

> > And there it was, a small bit of information
> > encapsulated in the myths and legends
> > of these peoples who build this vessel

> > > His aversion to Kryptonians
> > > his cruel design / upbringing
> > > This beast can smell them out

> > Brainiac runs the probability charts numbers
> > and runs them across the paths of the universe

> > based on all information he can gather from surrounding
> > cultures data banks and star charts in 245,000 years the
> > remains of Doomsday are located in these coordinates

> After searching for 3 years he finds the creature in a loss of consciousness
> > floating in a decompressed ruptured hull of a space craft.
> > It is chained, bound with a technology beyond his capability.

> > > Damn after so many obstacles.

> > So in tow Brainiac returns his prize to our solar system
> > and hides it in a the asteroid belt between Jupiter and Saturn

> some device will open up this tin-canned disaster
> > chains cannot bind you for ever

> > > and hopefully once awake,
> > > you will smell your way to earth

> > and destroy Superman

Canto 87

200th anniversary of the Constitution
Congress overrides President Reagan's veto
of the Clear Air Act

reports condemn Reagan for Iran-Contra
Alan Greenspan appointed to head Federal
Reserve
Rev. Jim Baker resigns ministry in shame

Mike Tyson heavyweight champion
Wall Street stock crash
Andy Warhol dies

Superman & Lois in Love

And there are no clothes on this jungle island
A cape lies over a black slip, checkered skirt

Nothing to denote man from Superman
Hard nosed reporter from soft woman
There is man and woman, alone, whole

There is no communication in this part of the world.

The cargo ships pass sailing across the blue seas
Bringing bananas and spices to far away places

They live in a tree house, build fires and eat fish and fresh fruits
He gathers jungle flowers of reds, greens yellow
And she writes poetry and sketches in charcoal

There are no questions too great for this
placid setting, and before an open fire

great love consummated, flourishing
he opens, to her anything, everything

Have you ever had sex with a woman, is it different, I mean, you know,

Are you alone, lonely, Are you lonely over there, are you afraid of girls,

How do you save everyone all the time, is it work, a passion, a chain,

Is there an off time, how do you know when it is all over, have you hurt

ever killed in the line of duty
here he pauses, hesitates a
transitory transparent instant

Blue eyes glowing, admirably

I have never had to kill
to achieve any objective

There is always an elusive option,
that solution of empathy, concern

to neither win nor lose, a hovering point breaks even
between 1 and 0 : your needs met and people saved

You never come up against a greater enemy than your own potential

And Lois Lane and Superman lie before the campfire
she places a soft hand on his cheek, never have I met

anyone like you, your beautiful heart and caring eyes

who will protect your precious soul
my beloved, I want you so much to be mine,

like this, all the time, I would give it all up for you
and you would for me as well,

but we wouldn't would we,

I need and the world needs you in it
If for nothing else than to dream on your wings

speaking of which, your paradise isn't so
perfect, there is no coffee here, maybe we

could see if we can have a Starbucks
franchised out in that second tree from the left

Flying in the evening sun they spot a strange star flying in the distant.

what is that to thee?

What is the proper noun for that blinding emotion of loss

    someone so special to you that your very cells trumpet
    curl cheeks to smiles, a kiss as a kiss, as time goes by,

        first you want to scream, then maybe hit the plaster wall
        after that hurts the hands you begin to well with tears red
        hysterical chokes of no no no it cannot be, not that quickly

        not now

        lost to us all but one, who is always composed reminds
        how things will be alright, this is natural, a better place
        and they are happier now. Cruelty beyond acceptance

        cruel in letting go with nothing more to do, the interest
        changes to responsibility and that is kit and kin to work

        The searches across great plains, white fog, yellow weeds
        if you follow death will he remember you for your devotion
            if you plead will he grant your wish
            take me instead, I am nothing

            with without
            take me, not

    bodies that we throw around in love seems so frail when bleeding
    if you tape it then maybe, place this bone back in right, pray tears

    There is no logic only time
    time to dwell on moments past

    look for that presence in things not dusted, restrained

    (you always knew she would get away but you are never prepared
    when it happens it is all that consumes and routines cease, flouting
    what should have happened this day, that odd dentist appointment

        make sure you close the bank accounts
    and don't advertise the funeral, you might get burgled when away

    one must know joyous possession before …

Canto 88

Bush is elected President
                              terrorist bomb 747 over Lockerbie,
          Scotland

Lt. Col. Oliver North indicted in Iran-Contra Affair
                    FAX machines

severe drought strikes the agricultural midsection of the
country
                              DuPont announces it will stop
                    producing CFCs

Tele-evangelist Jimmy Swaggart caught up in moral scandal
Phantom of the Opera leads comeback of Broadway Theater

A red eye initiates a flicker

Back to Brainiac

Where there is life there is hope; 2 miles below the surface
the computer that is Brainiac hums, projecting a hologram

to the imaging, we will rendezvous in orbit at 0245, you have your orders fulfill them

          over head of the NASA laboratory in Huston, Texas
          the projection of Brainiac breaks through the ceiling
          in an outlying warehouse, using a laser cannon, beaks

          in and sees his prize the superstring oscillating ion torch,
          able to cut at the atomic level, is reputed to cut through
          damn near anything. Brainiac attaches anti gravity robots
          removes it and carries it off into space: it is 0150, soon 0245

          rushing with his equipment to meet the central processing unit
          they join and set a course for the asteroid belt and Doomsday

          Lights the torch and begins to cut the chains that restrain,
          bind this evil in one place for millennia, the stories, myths
          I've read, if this is correct, is the answer so long eluded

The greater the potential the greater the foe

          And as it cuts Brainiac laughs at his fortune.
          the chains begin to break, tear at the seams,
          and something unexpected cracks.

          A red eye initiates a flicker, then bolts open.
          Brainiac falls back in fright. It is awake, alive.
          And the loosen chain, cracks, breaks open

          freeing one arm, and grabs out and clutches life,
          clutches Briainic by the servo, breaking it and he hangs
          there limp, dangling from the left hand of death. Swings
          the body aside and smells the empty space.

Ahh to be alive again.

But what is that? After so long ….
The scent is coming from that blue planet.

that is where to go.

Flying in the evening sun this spot becomes a strange star flying in the distant.

The chain of death assembles in conception, in gloom
nature of tooth and bone, excited by power the imagination
floating across the ear and eye, he was a light grey, wisps
of white hair, bright red eyes, a tiny jagged smile, in conception,

in gloom

and immediately three axioms are fulfilled. Perception, form
of an outward generating spiral that will end, an upper limit,
regenerate into a new perception/conception of atmosphere,
from high atop a tower, a form following of content, so to say,
from a reborn voice, no matter its nature of tooth and bone.

in doom

If you love me let me know for Ultimately, the beginnings
of cycles are in the endings; Doomsday has crossed stars
meeting valiant attacks and challenges all ending in failure,
smashed with bone all hopes; there was never anything left

here relation to death is a matter of business, the corruption
and pollution of honor constituting an obstacle to action,

lost through space in the remains of a rocket
a crime against its own purpose

Doomsday pushed off for the blue planet in Brainiac's ship
there were no controls only propulsion, it hurdled in mania

Flung past Mars, just misses the moon and is redirected downwards
by an orbiting telecommunications satellite, the blackout
is felt immediately in the western world, no connections

CNN started broadcasting on what little information was available

On a balcony of palm trees Superman and Lois look into the evening sun
they spot a strange star flying in the distant. Uses his super sight sees
what it is "I was afraid this day would come. We must go now"

immediately they took flight for home

subsequently only chasing destruction

Canto 89

US Forces capture Pres. Manuel Noriega for drug
trafficking
Supreme Court OKs Flag burning
major earthquake in Northern California shakes up a
World Series game Pete Rose banned from
Baseball.
Exxon Valdez Oil Spill

Cold War ends

Newsroom

And it was not long after Doomsday emerged from inside the Earth
    did he begin moving towards Metropolis
    homing in on the scent of the Kryptonian

Superman, destroying everything on his path, buildings were broken,
    cars upturned, on fire and exploded, smoke filled buildings,
    gas fires and electrical lines down, bridges swayed in his step

    what are we without electricity and heat, connections

    As the reports of a rampaging monster came over CNN
    the Justice League of America set out to stop the beast

    Alex Popofitinalfolous was on scene when Doomsday
    took on the JLA team Maxima, Bloodwynd, Booster Gold,
    Fire, Ice, Guy Gardner, Blue Beetle II

        and won
        one arm tied behind his back

            Doomsday came to earth
            wearing a restraining jacket

            clasping one arm
            behind his back!

Doomsday didn't stop his attack
each member, each hero left for dead

Blue Beetle, sadly is seriously injured
Booster Gold damaged beyond repair

through this battle, in his race for earth Doomsday's
restrains were loosened and he proceeds to destroy

as he walks across, wait a minute, it looks like

what is that in the sky … it's

            It is at this moment, now
            Superman joins the fight

Canto 90

Iraq invades Kuwait
Bush commits troops to Persian Gulf
Oliver North's Iran-Contra convictions
overturned
US sends aid to Russia

Bush raises taxes in spite of famous
Read My Lips, No New Taxes
Robert
Mapplethorpe's
photography
Hubble telescope doesn't work

Superman enters into the fight

Okay, I'm here now, I'll handle it.

with an air of finality confused scared fear falling by

Doomsday was created as the perfect killing being
He would absorb life through death

You will never come up against a greater foe
than your own potential, this may be more

Superman knowing all things that should come upon him,
went forth, flying over the broken cement city block,

called from above, Doomsday, Whom do you seek?

For a moment the creature stopped, lay down the steel I beam it was swinging
lifted it nose into the wind, taking a great deep breath, smelled yesterday's foe

through white teeth it growled, Are you the Kryptonian?

Superman answered, I am he:

since you seek only me
let them go, unharmed

Superman vowed to himself when he began as a hero
that he would never take a life, to save one yet loose another
was unacceptable, there was no option he could not conceive

even if he could kill Doomsday, what would Doomsday return as

Superman fought as a hero
along side of the JLA

and with their combined strength took on foes greater than galaxies

> the fierce battles
> the long hot fights

but our heroes were losing

together they might be able to stop Doomsday!
> but our heroes were losing, together

> To die away as if a divine irony, a practical joke
> all their mighty powers managed to free Doomsday's
> other arm unleashing the full of his power.

And with this the last of the heroes ran out of breath,
Superman stopped for a moment, on a building top,

thirsty, his arm hurt but was not broken. He looked over the battle field to see
all of the city in ruins, buildings halved at stairways, sewer lines ruptured,

> black water gave rise to grey smoke, a trumpet
> it came down to just Superman and Doomsday!

> Superman is held high over Doomsday's head
> is thrown through a blacktop street,

> must match his speed, his strengths

> Superman's outfit torn, red blood dripping
> outlining muscles thought impenetrable

>> He fights back, grasping onto the razors and horns
>> of Doomsday's leg, he spins and tossed it high into the air

>> and up into the air, fists for ramming, plows into the beast,
>> knocking it as baseball to bat, far out field, into the seas

For now a moment to rest, it will be back, need a better plan

>> But that moment was shorter than expected.
>> The creature bounced back, leaping forth from
>> the waters, taking flight in a bound back with life

>> greater than when had left.
>> Superman knew it was time

More buildings collapsed as they threw each other through,
cars thrown, buses overturned, people terrified though none

hurt by the cunning of our hero, his valor held in confidence
How could anything happen to Superman. CNN helicopters
on scene for what parts of america could still see,

> Superman was feeling his life fading
> in and out and in,
> thought at any moment he might die

>> Doomsday, too was well matched in his pain
>> no other had withstood him this far, however,
>> Doomsday, would return and learn from this one

Superman fought as hard as a hero could
but he knew if this Doomsday killed him

there would be no one left

there would be no one left to withstand his assault

                       Superman must stop Doomsday

at all costs!

He summoning all strength he had and continued to fight!

      the entire Earth was in peril
      he must break his first oath

      taking a life to sacrifice everything
                  to save everything

      put every bit of his power and strength into one punch.

      He and Doomsday collided: feed my lambs

Choosing his own! feed my sheep
Superman committed himself to saving

Choosing his own! in self sacrifice: feed my sheep
so hard it sent a shock wave across the entire city!

                  Dark as day, Doomsday was dead.

Canto 91

Operation Desert Storm

US defeats Iraq
Clarence Thomas wins confirmation to the Supreme
Court
Savings and Loan scandal
the beating of Rodney King
Pan Am and Eastern Airlines go out of business
Jeffrey Dahmer confesses
Biosphere II
basketball star Ervin *Magic* Johnson announces he is
HIV positive
Navy Tailhook scandal.

Chicago Bulls led by Michael Jorden win their first
NBA championship

Around America

On television, a CNN commentary:

it is expedient that one man should die for the people, it's the ultimate heroics
and in living rooms across the land people threw their Dada cola at the screen

I spoke openly to the world;
in secret have I said nothing.

On the streets bearing his cross went forth into a place called the place of a skull

Then Doomsday took Superman, and scourged him.
his mother Martha Kent, Jimmy Olsen, and Lois Lane.
watched helpless in the ensuing conflict

Lois to Jimmy : You must help him, you are his best friend!

Mrs. Lane, if Superman is having difficulties here,

what can I do?
what can any of us do but watch and cry

and immediately the cock crew.
Great Caesar's Ghost, cried Perry White

and far from the battle people gathered to look upon their homes, their lives saved
so far from it all, yet intertwined within the sorrow, one woman finds a torn piece of
Superman's cape, she holds it close to her face, wipes her tears in the rag

Canto 92

Bill Clinton elected President
                                 US troops sent to Somalia
Manuel Noriega is convicted in Florida
                               Oregon Senator Bob Packwood meets
          sexual harassment
                           Johnny Carson retires
Dan Quayle takes on *Murphy Brown*
boxer Mike Tyson convicted of rape
Joe Shuster dies at age 78 on July 30

Superman #75

Death of Superman

Dark as day, Doomsday was dead.

… Horror of all horrors what has it taken in its wake

his mother Martha Kent, Jimmy Olsen, and came near the body.
He choked for water, and Lois Lane gathered him up into her arms,
her husband, his blood on her skirt and arms, clutching the cape
of the fallen hero making fast bandages, trying to prevent, stop

When Superman saw his mother, he whispered "Woman, behold thy son!
                        Then said he turned to Lois, Behold thy mother!

After this, Superman knowing that all things coming to an end,
The people were safe. It is finished: and he bowed his head,
         and died quietly in the arms of his true love Lois Lane.

Then Conchubar, the subtlest of all men,
Ranking his Druids round him ten by ten,
Spake thus: "Cuchulain will dwell there and brood
For three days more in dreadful quietude,
And then arise, and raving slay us all.
Chaunt in his ear delusions magical,
That he may fight the horses of the sea.
'The Druids took them to their mystery,
And chaunted for three days.
         Cuchulain stirred,
Stared on the horses of the sea, and heard
The cars of battle and his own name cried;
And fought with the invulnerable tide.

                                    W.B. Yeats

Canto 93

Terrorist bombing of World Trade Center
abortion clinic murder of Dr. David Gunn
White House Aide Vincent Foster commits suicide
Attorney General Janet Reno sworn in
don't ask, don't tell policy
NAFTA
Internet
David Koresh
Branch Davidian's die in standoff with ATF

And what does one do to save the life of the greatest hero know,
thought impervious to all things, one cannot use CPR, or attach an IV

We deal with the grieving process in many different ways,

our Superman is gone.

And after this a dear friend of Superman,
took away the body on the outskirts of town
to Arimathea Labs
under cover of night,

and brought a mixture of myrrh, aloes, chemicals and radiants,
Taking the body of Superman, wound in linen clothes
with the spices and elements

In the place where he was killed there was a garden;
and in this garden was built a mausoleum out of gold

and there laid Superman

A statue was placed at the base of the man in cape
with an eagle perching on his right arm

Superman, the Hero of the World
Remember him always, in peace

Lois Lane visited the tomb nightly
fearing the emptiness of their home

One Tuesday, Lois came to the tomb,
The golden door wide open, lights on

She went in and it was empty,
She ran out, and screamed

The Batman and Robin responded
immediately, they too took comfort
in visiting this place

What have you done with him?
finger pointing screams at them

Lois you have to calm down, what happened
Damn it Bruce, she falls in his arms crying

How?

And so it was they entered the tomb and the crystal coffin was empty

Maybe there are things at work we don't understand

And there are also many other things which Superman did, the which, if
they should be written every one, I suppose that even the world itself could
not contain the books that should be written.

Superman, the Hero of the World
Remember him always, in peace

Canto 94

Ice skater Nancy Kerrigan attacked by associates of her competitor
Tonya Harding
>   major earthquake in Los Angeles
>   Kurt Cobain's suicide
>   O. J. Simpson accused of murder

Susan Smith drowns her own children and blames a fictional black car-
jacker
>   Michael Jackson marries Lisa Marie Presley
>   CIA agent Aldrich Ames caught working for the
>   Russians
>   young American caned in Singapore

Richard Nixon and Jacqueline Kennedy Onassis die.
>   assault weapon ban
>   Gary Larson retires
>   serial killer John Wayne Gacy executed

>   Jeffrey Dahmer murdered in prison

For fears of what to do with the remains of Doomsday
the scientists were at a loss, but agreed to send the remains
to the core of a class 7 star in the next galaxy.

>   A rocket was constructed
>   the thing thrown in and shot off

How cheer you now, creature from beyond
our negative has cancelled out our positive
may your remains smolder in a super nova

The voice calls out to the poet
the acceptance and rejection.

ethereal high and lonely melody
the poet is blinded by eternal beauty only to have it wander away

>   But then,

>   wait … a twinge

>   a red eye initiate, stirs

233

A prodigy who obtained his Literature degree while still in his teens, Geoffrey Gatza was a gifted poet, whose inability to work within the system led him outside of established literary circles. As the "Midnight Poet," Gatza used his great wealth, talent and formidable network of contacts to provide Avant Garde poetry for a wide range of readers for whom orthodox poetry had failed.

While investigating the influx of a new and dangerous bio-mimetic languages, Gatza was infected with mutagenic viruses which interacted randomly with other chemicals in his bloodstream. As a result, Gatza lost his vision except while using special goggles of his own creation.

It has been speculated the energy Gatza received from his father was the catalyst for his insanity but this is not entirely true. Something else has been infecting his mind ... something very powerful. Gatza has dedicated himself to protecting the downtrodden of his city from a continuing series of deadly poetic schemes by the insidious School of Quitetude.

Geoffreygatza.com | Blazevox.org | editor@blazevox.org

Author's Endnote:

I am beginning the final draft of this project on September 21st, 2001. Tonight is the unprecedented multi-broadcast telethon, America: Tribute to Heroes. It is a fitting responsible reaction, no less than a super-media spectacular in its own right, seeking support of America through unified entertainment. Tonight is a lonely night. Blaze, my cat, friend, and advisor is spending the first night away from my side since our relationship began. She dislocated her shoulder and is in deep pain. We were turned out of the clinic for lack of money. We walked home in the rain, limping, alone and destitute. I gave the last of my money and I cared nothing about me, only her. I cried for her, for her poor little arm, which was just dangling there. I was most afraid that she would have to be put to sleep. But no … she is a strong little meow. She kept me alive last year. She is my hero. I am reeling in her absence. As I type she sits and edits as we go. But tonight my muse is not here. And I must find strength from something, and even as the TV is as much a family member as my cat, it is nothing compared to sleep with dull purr and a lick on the nose. These are the values I uphold. All actions are driven by reactions from fear and love, or a primal combination of both. Tonight it is Clarice and TV, my family; my family is hurting. We became separated the night of President Bush's famous speech, right when Trent Lott looked human. Is this an omen of things to come? Last week we, as a nation, were attacked by unknown terrorists. The week before there was a certain sense of freedom that was going to make itself known in this poem, but that cannot be regained. Freedom yesterday, freedom tomorrow, but never freedom today. This attack will undoubtedly effect the production of art. It would be nice to be able to indulging in language and its meaning verses its affective nature. This poem was always intended to be more than parody of heroic narrative. More than a flippant depiction of a nation trying to buy a hero while settling on market testing of the next big trilogy the likes of Rambo, Dirty Harry, and Darth Vader. Americans love conflicted heroes. And it is this reason I choose Superman. He is the only true hero to fly through three quarters of the 20th century, being written by many different writers with very different motives and attributing specific powers that were relative to their age. He is a social democrat that never takes a life, never fights with vengeance, never uses too much force than needed. He out thinks his enemy, using their character weakness to defeat them. This method leaves us admiring his arm folded smug smirk to signify his victories. His devotion to humanity is odd, as he is not human. An alien who embodies all things humans wish to be able to do. To fly without the fears of Icarus, to lift a weightlifter lifting his maximum, to have x-ray eyes … to be able to save everyone all the time and never loose sight of his goals. And, he never swears. He is written to be the symbol of hope and the protector of all things that are humanity. We are all one. We are all at one with ourselves and we cannot bring ourselves to love one another. Tonight, we need a hero; and tonight I choose Superman. Tonight, alone, I write a tale for all ages. It is a basic tale of human victory, sacrifice and bravery. It is a tale told by an idiot swept away with his fear. And it is fear, that demon nothing, that comic book heroes fight every issue, every month.

Ever Forward,
Geoffrey Gatza

September 21, 2001
Buffalo, NY

Made in the USA